How To Create And Sell NFTs
— A Guide For All Artists

Magnus Resch
& Tam Gryn

Index

- 4   Introduction
- 26   NFTs under criticism
- 44   Data Studies – Research Findings
- 68   Mint an NFT
- 96   How to build a Web3 Community
- 126   The Future
- 146   Conclusion
- 152   Further Reading & References
- 162   Experts

●Intro-
duction●●●

Introduction

● In March 2021, a work by an American artist known only as "Beeple" sold for a staggering $69.3 million, making Everydays: The First 5000 Days one of the most expensive works by a living artist. The sales price alone made this transaction remarkable but there was something more. ●●

●1.1●● Introduction

This unprecedented price left many in the conventional art world bewildered. How could a JPEG file created by an obscure artist without significant gallery representation or museum shows sell for millions of dollars? And what Christie's had sold was not typical of digital artwork. This record-breaking transaction was for the purchase of a non-fungible token (NFT).

Technically, it was a computer file, a JPEG, with nothing tangible about it. However, it was more than simply a digital file. The digital artwork was sold as an NFT—a digital proof, you could call it—which facilitated not only the certification of the item's uniqueness but also an ongoing record of the work's ownership history. This token ensured that the work could never be edited or modified and that no replica of the work could ever be passed off as authentic, since any reproduction would lack the original's distinctive identifier.

> Think of yourself as a pioneer. The space is limitless; no idea is too big. GIANNI LEE, ARTIST

Something very important had just occurred that had the potential to change the function of ownership in the art world: a JPEG could be

Introduction

sold for millions since the associated NFT acted as the custodian of its uniqueness. The problems posed by counterfeits and lack of provenance (ownership history) would vanish overnight through the use of art NFTs. The owner of a work could now sell it at any moment, with complete confidence in the transaction. And the faith of buyers with respect to the legitimacy of their purchases would increase. No longer would costly expert opinions be needed to verify the authenticity of a work, and sales could happen within seconds, leaving out auction houses and galleries. And finally, artists could become millionaires overnight—circumventing galleries, museums and top collectors. It felt like a new dawn had come upon the sleepy art world.

> Use the technology around you to show your heart to the world in ways that have never been done before. FEWOCiOUS, ARTIST

No surprise, therefore, that shortly after the Beeple sale, an increasing number of artists began to contact us, asking, "What about me? How can I tap into these new income streams? How can I begin an NFT project? What about resale royalties? Are NFTs here to stay or merely a money-making scheme? And what exactly are NFTs, the blockchain, and cryptocurrencies?"

This book will give you the answers and help you start your own NFT project. We will share five essential lessons to set you on your way to achieving your goals:

- We will explain the fundamentals of NFTs, the blockchain, the metaverse and cryptocurrencies.

- We will provide a market overview of the NFT space and compare it to the traditional art market.

- We will analyze why some NFT projects are successful and others aren't.

- We will explain how best to sell your NFTs.

- We provide further reading material so you can stay up to date on future developments in the space.

Magnus Resch is widely considered to be the leading expert on the art market. He is a professor of art management, currently lecturing at Yale University. He has taught previously at Columbia University, University of St. Gallen, Luxembourg School of Business, and Zagreb School of Economics and Management. Ever since NFTs first appeared on the scene, Magnus has been closely following developments and collecting NFTs and has been interviewed by leading people in the field. His journey in the art market started when he was 20 years old when he ran a gallery. He then wrote his PhD in art economics and, to date, has published seven books on the art market, including three bestsellers. His most recent book is *How To Become A Successful Artist*. Magnus is also the founder of two art internet companies: Larryslist.com, the world's leading art collector database, and Magnus.net, an app that works like Shazam for art, with Leonardo DiCaprio as an advisor and investor. He can be found at @magnusresch on all social media platforms.

> Initially, authenticity and uniqueness – does the art feel authentic to the creator and does it stand out in a crowded market? Subsequently, success is about building relationships with peers and collectors and being cognizant of supply and demand. ERIC YOUNG, COLLECTOR

Tam Gryn is one of the key drivers in the crypto art and NFT spaces. She is the former director of fine arts at Rally.io, where she helped artistic communities create their own autonomous crypto economies. She is also the head curator at SHOWFIELDS, a contributor to the BanklessDAO and Friends With Benefits, and has lectured at Harvard Business School, as well as the New York Academy of the Arts. She was formerly the head of the curatorial department of the Artist Pension Trust and head curator for RAW POP UP. Tam has curated multiple art exhibitions and charity fundraisers. Clients and collaborators include Brooklyn Museum, Whitney Museum, McCann Worldgroup, La Biennale di Venezia, UTA, Glossier, Heineken, Evian, and Mastercard. Originally from Venezuela, Tam studied art history at Sorbonne University, politics at Reichman University, and negotiation at Tel Aviv University. She can be found at @tamgz on her social media accounts.

> Choose your NFT art niche, build your community and be active in it. Even if it takes time, don't give up. KAREN LEVY, COLLECTOR

Introduction

As you can see, we have both been involved in the crypto space for several years and see ourselves as early adopters of NFTs. But we are also deeply rooted in the traditional art space, understanding the role of artists, and their needs. We are passionate about the possibilities that NFTs offer to the art community but also conscious of their limitations and risks. It's this passion to support artists, as well as wanting to be involved early in the development of a nascent technology, that has motivated us to write this book. Our approach is based on a triangle of ideas, as follows.

> Think hard about what NFTs do for your practice both conceptually and practically before you dive in—Know the limitations of the technology and do your best to parse the reality from the hype. Whether the goal is to generate buzz with subversive art, or to create a sustainable annuity through secondary resale royalties be sure you know who your market is and whether they are likely to purchase NFTs. SARAH ODENKIRK, LAWYER

We rely on data. Although we comprehend the history, intricacies, and complexities of the conventional and NFT markets, we focus on market information and bottom-line data rather than personal stories or art historical annotations. In a market that has proven to be very complicated, anecdotal evidence has a role, but it also has limits. As you will see in the next chapters, this book is founded on research studies and extensive study of best practices as opposed to personal thoughts or trials.

We look at the art market from a global perspective. In a global market, understanding the global context is vital. Tam grew up in Venezuela and studied and worked in Paris, Tel Aviv, and New York, and presently lives in Miami while teaching and curating globally. Magnus, who resides in New York City, was born in Germany, attended Harvard, Stockholm, and the London School of Economics, completed his doctoral dissertation in Hong Kong, and taught (among other places) in Croatia. The artists we interviewed for this book are from every continent.

> Use all your senses to engage. Hang out in Discord, go to events, connect, listen, learn, act. NOAH DAVIS, YUGO LABS

We listen—obsessively and intently—to experts in the field. We conducted over 100 interviews with prominent NFT specialists for this book. This has greatly assisted in ensuring that our results are relevant and validated by industry leaders. We met with NFT artists, collectors, marketplace entrepreneurs, journalists, influencers, museum directors, and market researchers. The views of these professionals contribute to a broader understanding of the NFT sector and give this book richness and depth. Some of these talks took place on Magnus's Instagram and Twitter accounts and Tam's Twitter. Information from these sources has made its way into the book in the quotations that you can see on each page.

This book provides recommendations to stimulate and direct your ideas while initiating an NFT project, but we make no guarantee. Some ideas may not be suitable for your project, some may need modification, and others may already be outdated as the space is evolving so quickly and technology is adapting. You are responsible for determining the applicability of our advice to your practice. And you will also encounter successful initiatives that have taken a different path. We don't claim to possess all of the answers. However, in our opinion, the following pages provide an outline of the most effective and replicable strategy. We hope it gives you a whole new perspective on NFTs and inspires you to see their potential benefits for you and your career.

> First and foremost, you should be a buyer yourself. In collecting, you meet other members of the community and gain different perspectives that will influence your own work and positioning. We're still so early, no one can confidently say they know it all - which is great! It's ripe for making mistakes and that's the only way you learn and grow. MIKE DARLINGTON, MONSTERCAT

Introduction

●1.2●●

Blockchain, NFTs, Web3 - The Basics

Cryptocurrency, NFTs, Ethereum, Web3, blockchain, tokens, the metaverse—a lot of words have been flying around in the past couple of years. Whatever the starting point, we think that all artists need to know how NFTs have the potential to transform their abundance. First, some very basic definitions before we dive in. NFTs are digital "tokens" associated with the sale of artworks and memorabilia. Blockchain is the technology that underpins NFTs. Ethereum is an example of a cryptocurrency that can be used to purchase an NFT. With blockchain, the ownership history of a piece is baked into the item itself—and is accessible to anyone. Imagine if you could look at any artwork and immediately know every person who had ever owned that work. Sounds futuristic, but blockchain and NFTs allow us to get there. And, finally, the metaverse can mean anything but is currently most often used as a fancier word for "cyberspace." If this was too much content, too quickly, and the key ideas are still unclear to you, don't worry. Let's take a step back now and look at the main terms in detail.

> Be a part of Web3. Make use of the technology and community in the creation of your art. DEREK ANDERSON, METRA

Blockchain

Although cryptocurrencies and NFTs attract all the fanfare, they would be nothing without blockchain technology. Standard definitions will tell you that a blockchain is a ledger that is digital and distributed. This simply means that electronic records are maintained not in a single place (such as in a physical record book or on a server) but spread over many computers. New information is added to the ledger in parcels called "blocks," over time resulting in a chain of blocks draped over a network of multiple computers that verify, approve and store data. Think of it as a pearl chain: every time a transaction is done, another pearl is added to the chain.

The beauty of the system is that new blocks are added to the chain only when there is a majority consensus among the existing computers that the new transaction information is valid and there is no fraud detected. Because the transactions are irreversible, this takes away a potential avenue for fraud, as well as the need to rely on a trusted third party. Blocks are added using cryptography, which involves the computation of complex mathematical problems, thus giving the blockchain what is commonly referred to as its "immutability"—the record of transactions on the ledger is permanent and unable to be changed.

> **Consider NFTs as a medium, rather than a digital representation of physical work.**
> CAROLINE TAYLOR, APPRAISAL BUREAU

As transactions are added to the blockchain, it increases in size, meaning there are more eyes on the ledger. The way it's designed, each node contains information about the entire chain. The blockchain is effectively a database spread over a network where every participant can see everything, including attempts by any party to tamper with a block. Hacking one block will not alter the information in the rest of the ledger, meaning it cannot be hit by malicious cybercrime in the same way individual computers or whole networks can be compromised.

If all of this was too technical, maybe this helps as a takeaway: Blockchain is a highly secure system that doesn't allow forgery or fraudulent behavior, and that cannot be hacked, as it can be seen by every participant of the blockchain. This system contains a history of time-stamped, irreversible transactions, and it doesn't have a single point of input.

Bitcoin and other currencies

So, now that we have a basic understanding of what a blockchain is—a self-preserving, self-managing, tamper-resistant electronic ledger that everyone who wants to can see—let's talk about cryptocurrencies. Most probably, you will have heard about Bitcoin, but perhaps not so much

Introduction

> If you add value before you ask for value, you will never have to ask. DAVE KRUGMAN, ARTIST

about Ethereum, Solana, Avalanche, Tezos and the many other cryptocurrencies floating around. And, unless you're a digital artist or naturally curious about such things, chances are that *all* you know about Bitcoin is that it is a cryptocurrency. Whatever that is.

What exactly is a cryptocurrency? The best way to answer this question is to compare it to traditional currency. We will use Bitcoin as our example. Unlike cash, Bitcoin:

→ Is not physical.
→ Cannot be counterfeited.
→ Cannot be stolen in the same way that cash can.
→ Is not worth what the government says it's worth. Buyers define its worth.
→ Cannot be devalued by the creation of more Bitcoins because there is a fixed amount. No more bitcoins can be added.

There are also some similarities between Bitcoin and cash. One major similarity—which will become important in the discussion of NFTs later in this book—is that, like traditional currencies, cryptocurrencies are "fungible": if you own a Bitcoin, it is worth the same as anyone else's Bitcoin.

Bitcoin was the first cryptocurrency. It was introduced in 2009 in a paper published by "Satoshi Nakamoto," likely a pseudonym. The paper proposed a new way of conducting electronic transactions that would eliminate the need for trusted third parties such as banks. "Nakamoto" introduced the paper with a statement that sounded very technical.

> Trust in your work. If you really love the world you are creating, then others will meet you in that realm. IX SHELLS, ARTIST

Indeed, the topic is very technical, but closer examination shows the immense benefits that cryptocurrency can have for virtually everyone—including artists.

● "What is needed is an electronic payment system based on cryptographic proof instead of trust, allowing any two willing parties to transact directly with each other without the need for a trusted third party.... In this paper, we propose a solution to the double-spending problem using a peer-to-peer distributed timestamp server to generate computational proof of the chronological order of transactions." ●●

Translation: "Nakamoto" is proposing a system of electronic payment from art collector to artist that does not involve any intermediary. Banks—and galleries—and the associated costs that come with them (e.g., the 50% revenue split) will become irrelevant. Also, the possibility of fraud, unauthorized copies and the question of authenticity (think Salvador Mundi, Knoedler Gallery and unauthorized Warhol prints) are eliminated by the proof provided by the system.

> Your community is your most important asset. GMONEY, COLLECTOR

NFTs

A basic understanding of the blockchain and cryptocurrency are important when it comes to grasping what NFTs are about. An NFT—a "non-fungible token"—is a digital record that can be used to represent an object with a value. The object could be physical (such as a painting, antique vase, baseball card or a ticket to a concert) or non-physical (such as music, video, a meet and greet with a sports star or celebrity, or a PDF or some form of digital artwork). Like cryptocurrency, NFTs rely on blockchain technology. But unlike cryptocurrency, which is "fungible" (i.e., your Bitcoin will always be worth the same as mine), NFTs are non-fungible, which is another way of saying that they are non-exchangeable. Each is a unique digital file with its own meaning and value.

> Be yourself, and do things on your own terms. This technology is in its early days, so comparing yourself to others when it comes to things like pricing, format and utility is only limiting yourself. ROXY FATA, INFINITE OBJECTS

Uniqueness, authenticity and scarcity are baked into NFTs. The utility of NFTs has only just begun to be explored. Any sector dealing with things that have value and can be owned, whether tangible or intangible, could potentially benefit from the application of NFTs. Creators of physical art, digital art and many other industries will benefit from the transformation that NFTs are bringing.

Introduction

Metaverse

"The Metaverse" is often mentioned in the same sentence as "NFTs" and "blockchain". It is difficult to understand the Metaverse, especially because it doesn't yet exist. Since Big Tech businesses such as Epic Games, NVIDIA, Microsoft, Intel, and Facebook (now referred to as "Meta") won't stop talking about it, it's worthwhile to investigate. According to Meta, "The metaverse is a set of virtual spaces where you can create and explore with other people who aren't in the same physical space as you. You'll be able to hang out with friends, work, play, learn, shop, create, and more."

> **Like any new tool or technology, your limit is your imagination - NFTs simply help you bridge new digital experiences.** MAURICIO FIGUEROA, META

Still not clear? Here's an exercise: In your mind, replace the word "Metaverse" with "cyberspace." Seldom will the meanings be significantly different. This is because the term relates not to a particular sort of technology but, rather, a wide (and often speculative) change in how humans engage with technology. It is uncertain if there will be a single metaverse or several distinct metaverses—or any metaverse at all.

Given that so many things may be the Metaverse, it is unsurprising that the term has been around for some time. It was originally used in Neil Stevenson's 1982 book *Snow Crash*. And it's been used in the context of Second Life, a popular online game with millions of active users that enables them to create avatars and live lives in a virtual environment. In the wake of the Covid-19 pandemic, the Metaverse has become a more widespread concept due to advances in blockchain technology and much of our work becoming more digital.

> **Focus on the art, not the money.** MELTEM DEMINORS, COINSHARES

Currently, the Metaverse is most often referred to in connection with digital real estate. Platforms such as Decentraland, Crypto Voxels, Sandbox, Mona, and Wilder World are virtual worlds where users can purchase "land" to build something on it or sell it later. For example, Sotheby's purchased land in Decentraland and has built a virtual gallery on it.

1.3
Web3

NFTs, blockchain, cryptocurrencies, the Metaverse—they all define aspects of what is often described as "Web3," another currently popular buzzword. The term is a reference to the evolution of the internet, which is currently on the cusp of its third major phase. It's worth understanding the three phases.

Web1: When the internet was created, we saw very static websites, portals, directories, email, chat facilities that improved our communication systems and marketplaces that sold physical goods. It was very low-bandwidth and hard to connect to, and the hardware to "dial up" was very limited. Companies such as Yahoo and Netscape created all of the content and value and fully benefited monetarily from it. We, as users, could only "read" these websites. We couldn't really participate or provide any value; we also did not own anything, and companies at that time did not own our data.

> Crypto Art is a movement of values over an aesthetic. If you want to be taken seriously, take the community and its values seriously. MARTIN LUKAS OSTACHOWSKI, ARTIST, HISTORIAN

Web2: There was a very clear shift in the early 2000s with the appearance of Facebook and other social media, and companies like Uber. All of a sudden, our technology expanded. Using widespread broadband internet, social networks and the cloud, we are no longer just readers in this economy. Users create a lot of the value that is showcased in these platforms. We upload our art, music, ideas, writing, photos, and products, and we work for some of these companies as freelancers. In other words, our content creates the value of the internet. But we don't monetize that content. That is, the benefits don't accrue to us—the companies and platforms are still the prime beneficiaries of the value that we upload to the internet. In Web2, not only do we "read"; we also "read and write." But companies own our creations and our data. This era is currently undergoing a transformation.

Web3: The blockchain is challenging the Web2 status quo. In Web3, we will live in a digital world that is dominated by technology, AI, bioengineering,

Introduction

sensors, wearables, AR/VR, 5G, space travel, space manufacturing, clean energy and, of course, crypto. Web3 allows users to monetize their contributions to the internet. Users are no longer satisfied with "likes" and followers in exchange for countless hours of unpaid work on social media. They want to not only "read and write" but also "own" their digital content.

> Own your own creative sovereignty by using your own smart contract. RICHERD CHAN, MANIFOLD

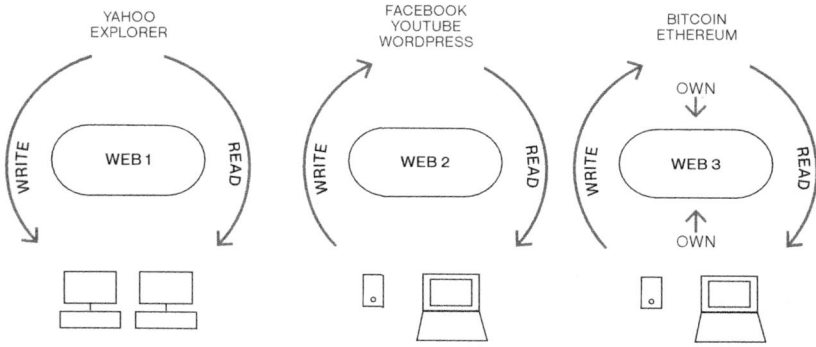

Ownership is the key concept of Web3. In Web2, whenever you upload a file, such as your art or a song or photo, the ownership of that file immediately transfers to the company that owns the platform. These companies then monetize the content by selling your data and content to advertisers who then feed you ads so that you purchase products from them. We are willing to accept this arrangement because the platforms allow us to upload and share our content easily and freely. These platforms have become power players in today's economy. Parts of the internet are now centrally controlled by a handful of Big Tech companies, such as Google, Meta, Amazon and Apple. Web3 attempts to change this by creating a decentralized form of the web so that creators of art, music and other content can own their data, as well as their own creations, in the form of digital assets. In a perfect scenario in Web3, the blockchain will maximize ownership, transparency, provenance, access,

> Web3 is a parallel universe in which all our creative ideas can come true. Become one with the technology available in this space. CORY VAN LEW, ARTIST

revenue streams, liquidity, patronage and collection.

For the art world, this could mean less dependency on galleries and art institutions that currently control transactions, ownership records, authentication and relationships. In Web3, artists—not the galleries, dealers or curators—are in control of their market. They decide who receives how much percentage of the project and they own the relationship with the buyer, set the terms and claim resale royalties.

Work hard, be nice and be patient.
WAGMI. AN RONG, SUPERRARE

Introduction

● 1.4 ● ●

Benefits for Collectors

So far, we have been talking rather abstractly about NFTs. So, what do art collectors really get when they buy an NFT? Here are some benefits:

Unique proof of ownership NFTs are a secure and unique proof of exclusive ownership. Essentially, the NFT authenticates, for all to see, that the collector is the owner of that art work.

> Don't hesitate to reach out for help, especially on Twitter; the NFT community is much more supportive than the traditional art community. ANNE MORGAN SPALTER, ARTIST

Proof of authenticity The NFT replaces a paper certificate of authenticity. The holder can show that the item is the original piece made by the creator.

Transparency The blockchain records the fact that you have purchased the NFT. It records who you bought from, who the previous owners were and what each party paid for it. Everyone has access to the history of the work, similar to what you see when you visit streeteasy.com, the New York City apartment purchase and rental site that tells you how much your neighbor is paying or what the previous tenant of your apartment paid.

A link to the artwork A link to the artwork is included with every NFT. It allows you to download the artwork and display it in any way you want.

> Follow your truest obsessions. Surround yourself with people whose work and behavior you respect. Support others as generously as you can, engage kindly, and contribute meaningfully. Be prepared to work really, really hard doing what you love, but take time to read, walk in nature, and surprise yourself. SASHA STILES, ARTIST

Utility Additional utility beyond simple ownership can be coded into the NFT. Value can be added by including a copy of the creator's signature, giving some form of exclusive access to the artist, providing early notification of events hosted by them, VIP tickets or special access. For example, some NFTs provide access to NFT-owner-only networking and community events and discussions (often held on Discord). Access to these exclusive benefits is lost once an NFT is sold.

A liquid asset An NFT can be sold directly to a buyer (assuming there is a buyer, of course). This can be done anytime, without the involvement of an intermediary. The marketplace that facilitates the transaction takes a small commission, similar to the fee a credit card company takes when their card is used..

As is the case in the traditional art world, owning an NFT does not give the owner the right to make copies or profit in some way from images of the art—unless the copyright to the object is transferred to the buyer and specifically recorded in the NFT file or in a written agreement. For instance, the NFT project Nouns is controlled under a Creative Commons "No Rights Reserved" license, which implies that anybody is permitted to use the "Nouns" name and characters in any context. It is available for public use. However, rather than relinquishing copyright, most artists are likely to be more interested in earning royalties from subsequent sales of the NFT—not just from the first sale—something made possible by the new technology and which has definitely not been the case in the traditional art world.

> Be creative and be daring. Forget about everything that already exists in the NFT space and allow your creativity to run wild. This is a young phenomenon and every project has been incredibly experimental to date. Follow in this way, as, after all, we're only at the beginning of the journey. I believe that the biggest project using this technology is yet to come. MICHAEL BOUHANNA, SOTHEBY'S

Introduction

● 1.5 ● ●

Benefits for Artists

The benefits for buyers are strong, as they eliminate some of the downsides of buying in the traditional art market. Artists benefit tremendously, as well. Here are some benefits:

A welcoming community Art galleries—and the art world, in general—can often be daunting to people not used to moving in those circles. Even artists may experience some of the snobbery and elitism of the establishment, depending on what part of the art scene they operate in and what "club" they belong to. The crypto art community is different, built as it is on collaboration and sharing. Most discussions on Discord, the platform used by many in Web3 to communicate, and Twitter are cordial, as communities built around NFTs are based on mutual interest and are democratic and welcoming.

Total control NFTs have flipped the script. If you have ever wondered if there was a better way of doing things than having to always go through art galleries and dealers to connect with and sell to your audience, here it is. Creators can now run the show and enjoy more control over the determination of value.

Royalties forever This is the real game changer. Artists can now create NFTs that are coded to allow them to receive royalties, meaning that all future resales, not just the first sale, will push a portion of the price back to the creator. Thus, if you sell a piece of art for $10,000 and ten years later it reappears on the market with an asking price of $10 million, you will earn a direct benefit of that increase in value. Actual numbers show this is happening. According to an analysis by venture capitalist a16z (Andreessen Horowitz), in the last year, NFTs paid out $174,000 per creator, while Facebook and Instagram paid out $0.10 per user, Spotify paid out $636 per artist, and YouTube paid out $2.47 per channel.

> If your aim is to make money, you wouldn't pick up a paintbrush. GABE WISE, GAC

Eco-friendly options You may be aware of concerns regarding the amount of energy consumed by bitcoin mining and cryptocurrencies in general, which is a problem in today's energy- and emissions-conscious world. These concerns are valid, but eco-friendly options exist and new options are appearing. Blockchains such as Solana, Polygon and Avalanche require far less energy and, thus, leave a smaller environmental footprint. Even Ethereum is currently moving to a greener proof-of-stake option.

Early mover advantage Throughout history, art has always developed through artists pushing boundaries, and they have often done that by pushing through the use of emerging technologies. Just as the invention of printing enabled artists to reach a wider audience and the advent of computers and then the internet spawned a seemingly infinite explosion of possibilities in terms of digital art and reach, NFTs represent another opportunity for a quantum step in the art world. Artists can now interact more intimately with their communities and sell their work (digital or physical) directly to buyers with no permissions required from a third party. Comparing the current state of adoption of Web3 to the development of the commercial internet we know, a16z places us at around 1995, many years before the formation of Web2 giants such as Facebook and YouTube.

> NFTs do not have to fit a certain mold. You can simply experiment and venture out into different expressions. Staying true to you will bring the best results.
> STUDIO DRIFT, ARTIST

Inspiration beyond the canvas "Digital art" no longer means only viewing a piece of art on a phone, tablet or computer. Technologies are emerging that enable digital art to be displayed in the physical world as holograms, on projection screens, or "printed" as a physical representation of the NFT (e.g., "Infinite Objects").

New audiences. And whales. An exciting new technology is attracting a new audience, many of whom would never have contemplated setting foot in an art gallery. We are seeing the emergence of "crypto whales," large crypto buyers whose transactions move markets. This new group of buyers embraces democratization, decentralization and permissionless art transactions. There are parallels with the Medicis and their influence on Renaissance art, but it remains to be seen if the whales are interested in political influence.

Introduction

Partnership between artist and audience Gone are the days when artists had to build relationships with their audiences through hours of unpaid effort—a labor of love in the hope of future revenue. If you have followers who value your art, NFTs can provide meaning through a sense of mutual ownership that benefits artists and their supporters financially, all while building and maintaining community.

Community connection Community is key. The success of NFTs depends on it, not only in the form of communities of collectors but also in opportunities for the formation of collaborations and collectives with other artists and direct engagements between buyers and artists. As it's so powerful, we've dedicated a chapter in this book to community building.

Be a leader Art snobs have always criticized those who have pushed the envelope. The names "Impressionism" and "Pointillism" were coined by critics who despised those movements. If you're criticized by the establishment for pushing the boundaries of art, you'll be in good company: the Impressionists, Duchamp, Warhol and Refik Anadol, to name a few. It is no coincidence that Sotheby's, Christie's and a few other leading galleries already accept cryptocurrencies as payment.

> This ecosystem rewrites the relationship between a creator and a collector; therefore, I strongly encourage artists to have a deeper relationship with those that support them. It is important to understand that many entities add value across the ecosystem. Please do not think that just because we have a way to directly engage and sell peer-to-peer, these institutions do not add value. Focus on creating, and outsource all the necessary aspects to be successful (e.g., PR, marketing, structure, accounting, getting closer to new collectors and events).
>
> PABLO RODRIGUEZ-FRAILE, COLLECTOR

Listing all these benefits can easily excite artists, and sometimes we find ourselves also dreaming of the endless solutions that Web3 and NFTs offer to the art world. To be clear, despite all the benefits that NFTs grant, we are also seeing the challenges and risks that come with them. Clearly, as an artist, you don't need to shift your practice from working with galleries, networking with curators and smooching with your existing buyers to only creating NFTs. Yet, we believe that a comprehensive understanding of NFTs, still in an early phase of their development, will put you in a commanding position to capitalize on opportunities as they arise.

As has always been the case in the world of art, it takes explorers, visionaries and inventors on the fringes to create and discover new ways to create and operate. But even in the art world, there is also fear, mistrust and apprehension of the unknown when those boundaries are pushed. Therefore, in the next chapter, we will address these criticisms to encourage you not only to find out for yourself how NFTs could transform art and the making and selling of it but also to understand their challenges and risks.

> Become an active participant in the space and buy work from others you admire to understand the ecosystem. Build relationships. Tell a story of you as the artist and the why behind the work you create. SPARKY, ARTIST

●NFTs under criti-cism●●●

● Many people in the conventional art community see NFTs as an untrustworthy get-rich-quick venture with no substance. The most common criticisms we hear are:

1) NFTs are not real art; 2) NFTs are ugly; 3) NFTs are bad for the environment; 4) It's a crypto bro's game. We will address each one of these concerns in this chapter. ●●

●2.1●● NFTs are not real art

If we take a deep dive into art history, we find that every single art movement that disrupted the status quo brought controversy with it.

In the late 19th century, as Impressionism was emerging, the painters who were involved in the developing movement were among the first to paint outside. At the time, it seemed absurd to bring a canvas to a field. Historically, artists had painted mostly for the church or royalty. Typically, art commissioned by the state for religious reasons was used for propaganda. However, this was just a portion of the issue; the aesthetic of Impressionism also generated heated criticism. The paintings were not realistic, and they deviated significantly from the aesthetic of Neoclassicism. They were "unclean." For many, Impressionist art was, beyond a doubt, "not art." It did not reflect the beliefs of society regarding the conventional church and the monarchy. There was no hierarchy. For some, though, Impressionist art signified their existence. In 1869, the establishment in Paris of new infrastructure, cafés and leisure consumption, including the opening of the first department store, led to a societal upheaval that was captured by Impressionist

> **Explore the medium. Enter it with no expectations to sell.** COLBORN BELL, MUSEUM OF CRYPTO ART

NFTs under criticism

paintings. People wanted contemporary aesthetics and consumerism. Artists no longer needed to make art with a societal message; they just wanted to create. Their "faulty illusions"—"impressions"—of nature and leisure, made only for the sake of painting, are now the focal points of fine art museums.

Another significant event in the history of the art world involved a pissoir. In 1917, the Society of Independent Artists received *Fountain*, a porcelain urinal signed by Marcel Duchamp,. The work was immediately greeted with hostility. Despite their support for democracy in art, the Society declined to exhibit the work because its members felt that exhibiting *Fountain* would degrade the other pieces on display. The Society's directors issued the following statement to the press: "The Fountain may be a very useful item in its place, but its location is not an art display, and it is not, by definition, an artwork." Why did the work inspire such animosity? Perhaps it was because the sculpture was intended to depict the culture of the times—the emergence of materialism and the age of the consumer. A prediction that humans would admire such items as art in the future was accurate, and *Fountain* and the thinking behind it influenced the exploration of similar notions. Duchamp set the groundwork for movements such as Pop Art. In 2010, the Andy Warhol Museum hosted "Twisted Pair: Marcel Duchamp/Andy Warhol," an exhibition examining the creative connections between the two artists. Warhol owned about 30 Duchamp works, including a reproduction of *Fountain*. Warhol realized that commercials, consumer products, newspaper photographs and people themselves could all be considered art. He recognized the ready-made, as well as the irony of mass manufacture. The iconic urinal was a jest, but it conveyed a kernel of truth that gave it generational cultural significance. Now, the work is regarded as a significant milestone in 20th-century art.

> **The features of the NFT space – the means of display, the speed of transaction, the methods of distribution – are distinct from the physical art world and must be considered critically and very practically. But ultimately, the main advice is to make art!! Real art! Good art!**
> SARAH MEYOHAS, ARTIST

Picasso was blamed for the fall of Western civilization by a 1938 article in the *Sunday Star*, a Washington, D.C., paper. Early reviews of Picasso blamed him for making women less attractive in his paintings. Picasso created Cubism, which represented new angles and perspectives;

his personal relationships and political activism, seen from different viewpoints, created a radical aesthetic for which society at that time was not prepared.

According to the definitions of society of his time, Andy Warhol's work did not pass as art. His work seemed to be merely a reproduction of advertising, indistinguishable from it. In the 1960s, Warhol was the first to realize the effect that consumerism and advertising would have on human behavior and society at large. Everything Warhol did has influenced artists of all disciplines who have followed after him.

Own the future. JESSE LEE, BASIC SPACE

No artist who has ever interrupted and altered the path of art history has done so without using "uncomfortable" aesthetics, nor was their work accepted without strident criticism. Yet the work of the Impressionists and Duchamp, Picasso and Warhol can be seen in art museums today. NFTs are following the same path as these previous disruptive art movements: nobody understood at first; all movements introduced unsettling aesthetics; and all developed in a bottom-up manner as a result of massive technological, economic, and societal shifts.

Digital Art History

To strengthen the argument that NFTs are part of art history, let's take a look at it. The Beeple sale at Christie's has made people sit up and take notice, but in fact, digital artists have been doing their thing since at least the 1960s, when a group of digital artists calling themselves "Algorists" explored the use of computer technology to generate art based on algorithms they coded. The term was coined by artist Jean-Pierre Hébert, members of this community included Roman Verostko, Frieder Nake, Vera Molnár and Manfred Mohr – names you might not be familiar with, but some of them have works in the MoMA.

In the decades that followed, digital art took on a variety of forms: video art, software art, augmented reality, virtual reality, artificial intelligence and, most recently, crypto art that uses the blockchain conceptually as a medium, kicked off in 2014 by Kevin McCoy and Anil Dash.

NFTs under criticism

They were working together for Rhizome's 2014 Seven on Seven initiative that paired artists with technologists. This collaboration introduced "monetized graphics" as a way of establishing ownership of digital work, with a view to protecting artists from exploitation and appropriation and giving them more control over their work, including the selling process. Their "proto-NFTs" aimed specifically to solve artists' problems rather than make money.

Sarah Meyohas, a conceptual artist, was another early adopter of the technology. In February 2015, five months before the introduction of Ethereum, she launched Bitchcoin, the first tokenization of art on the blockchain. Sarah went all in, working with her own proof-of-work blockchain and creating her own cryptocurrency. Another example is artist Eve Sussman, who explored the ideas of ownership and collaboration in her 2018 work *89 Seconds Atomized*. In this project, she broke up the final artist's proof of her 2004 short film *89 Seconds at Alcázar* into 2,304 unique blocks that could be collected, bought and sold, and reassembled anytime by the community of collectors if they wished to hold a viewing. Jennifer and Kevin McCoy's *Public Key/Private Key* (2019) involved the donation of a short film to Whitney Museum and the creation of a dynamic donor list by selecting 50 people from a pool of applicants. Each donor was given a digital certificate that could be sold, traded or gifted. The project explored and complicated the traditional museum–benefactor–audience relationship by making donorship a fluid process rather than one fixed by a single donation and memorialized by a plaque.

> The future of storytelling is in shared dimensional experiences, AKA: the metaverse(s), and anyone building there now will be light years ahead when mainstream adoption happens. AARON HUEY, ARTIST

These examples demonstrate that the art industry has been working with the concept of NFTs for some time; yet, it has not garnered much attention. Only in late 2017, the rare mix of an audience, new technology, and an abundance of crypto riches drove NFTs to the forefront of public attention. CryptoKitties, a game that allows users to own, breed and trade "kitties," saw tremendous growth and online buzz when the first cat was sold for $100,000. In the first few days, there was a rush in demand and sales of around $1 million. In December 2017, the game drew 10 percent of all Ethereum traffic, and the most expensive kitty sold for $170,000.

However, the game's popularity was short-lived owing to overstock, a widening wealth disparity between participants, and limits in blockchain technology. (The current value of a cat is around $28.)

While you may find it hard to take digital cats seriously, the reasons people bought them were no different from the reasons fine art buyers buy fine art. The images were aesthetically attractive and were fun to buy. They could be viewed as an investment because they appreciated in value. Participating in the game signaled to others that the buyer was on the leading edge of art and new technology and that they were "cultured" (at least in the online sense of that word), and it provided an outlet for personal expression while supporting the work of artists. Unlike fine art, however, CryptoKitties introduced something revolutionary that NFT brings to the table: the game and the art were accessible to virtually all, not just the wealthy.

> Follow the artists, creators, and builders that inspire you. DM them and start a conversation with them. Let them know why they inspire you and that you hope to connect or collaborate with them in the future. Don't ask for anything. Planting these authentic relationship seeds will provide the foundation for when you have something to say, offer, request, etc.
> DANIEL ROSENBERG, NOMAD BOULEVARD

As is the way with new opportunities, increased interest led to the development of new online markets, which, in turn, drew more people to join the action. CryptoKitties is no longer "The Big Thing." That honor has passed to NBA Top Shot, the NBA's platform for selling game highlights via NFTs. In Top Shot's first half-year, it generated revenue close to $400 million, heralding a new phase of accelerated interest in NFTs and skyrocketing sales.

The path from blockchain to NFTs continues to evolve. NFTs are altering the nature of art collecting as a business endeavor, particularly in terms of reselling artwork. In December 2021, the Singapore-based NFT investor Metakovan (who bought the $69 million Beeple piece) acquired 20 Beeple NFT artworks. Each item was a virtual work of art shown in a virtual museum and accompanied by a soundtrack. Metakovan's NFT fund, Metapurse, then divided the ownership of the works into tokens and sold them. Thousands of individuals purchased them, each effectively owning a portion of a digital artwork in a virtual museum and a portion of the associated music.

NFTs under criticism

●2.2●●

NFTs are ugly. I could do that

One can argue that aesthetics are subjective. What is objective, for the art institutions and markets that decide what is or is not worthy of the art history books, is context. Whether or not we personally like it, art is valuable only if it reflects a societal movement at the time and if it is presented in an accurate context. In the case of crypto art, the context is what we would call the "digitalization movement."

The world was subjected to digitalization at an accelerated speed during Covid-19 when we were forced to work from home and interact digitally more than ever. What started with experimenting with the Zoom background led eventually to artistic explorations. Some even created their own avatars as they were tired of always seeing their own faces on Zoom calls. Others played online games, transforming gaming into something larger than Hollywood and the North American sports industry combined. Crypto Art reflects this new phenomenon, too, accelerated by the adoption of blockchain technology in the form of cryptocurrencies and a realization of the function that NFTs could perform as a store of value or representation via a digital persona.

Take your time to create your work. Don't let the first thing you sell dictate what you do for the rest of your career. Signature style is a trap. PETER WU+, EPOCH GALLERY

While the digitalization movement has enabled Crypto Art, the Cypherpunk's Manifesto forms its underlying thesis. Drafted in 1993, the manifesto states a clear mistrust of governments, corporations and other large, faceless organizations.

The Crypto Art aesthetic that makes the conventional art world so uncomfortable is directly tied to society's adoption of digitalization, gaming and sci-fi utopian and dystopian behaviors. This nascent art movement is an ode to the decentralization, anonymity, and permissionless, bankless world-building and tech-reliant self-expression that celebrate the creators of blockchain infrastructure. Crypto Art is in context because it is true to its time and its identity and place. Of course, the Crypto Art movement has only just been born, but museums and institutions are now beginning to study and analyze the movement.

We understand that not every artist is part of this movement. We also understand that, to some, the concepts of avatars, decentralization, anonymity and criticism of the government seem far-fetched. Still, in order to understand the underlying context surrounding NFTs, we need to look in more detail at the characteristics of this movement. This will help to better explain the aesthetics we see reflected in the different categories of the Crypto Art movement today.

Animal Aesthetics = Avatars We see a lot of animals in the Crypto Art movement; there are apes, koalas, penguins, cats—the whole zoo. What is the obsession with animals? What does it mean? Animal representation is part of the avatar movement. Some claim that avatars in a potential metaverse represent your digital identity. In the physical world, the government dictates what is to be shown on our ID photos. In the digital world, avatars are all about self-expression and freedom to express one's identity and method of representation. Out of millions of options, we can select a unique NFT to represent us in the digital realm.

Futuristic Aesthetics = Cypherpunk Founders The Cypherpunk's Manifesto represents the foundation of crypto. The Cypherpunks were the first people to preach decentralization. They built the infrastructure that holds blockchain technology. They are a community of technologists that have been fighting the current banking and government systems anonymously for at least a decade now. This is their true aesthetic.

> Don't underestimate the power of sharing and documenting your process - it's important to provide as much context as you can so collectors and enthusiasts alike can connect with your work. SOFIA GARCIA, ARTXCODE

It's not surprising that one of the most successful NFT projects is called "Punks"—a clear reference to the founders.

Utopia versus Dystopia Aesthetics = The Specter of Centralization
Early adopters of crypto art see society at the crossroads. On the one hand, you have centralized companies like Meta who can build a metaverse using Web2 technologies, privacy logic, and your data. Imagine giving them the power of the blockchain and how they could potentially use their power to further control us. That could be a dystopia.

NFTs under criticism

The utopian system that Web3-native projects are trying to build would be decentralized. In such a scenario, artists would own their art and content and there would be autonomous communities with autonomous economies that traded assets amongst themselves without ads popping up everywhere.

Odes to the Blockchain Aesthetics = Historical Documentation Many NFT projects make use of not only avatars but also the symbols and logos of Bitcoin and blockchains. Whether they be Google Ethereum, Solana or Bitcoin, you will recognize their logos incorporated in artworks. This is similar to how religious art in Roman and Byzantine periods used votive images to represent the leading beliefs of the time. Symbolism is a language that we are accustomed to in the visual arts. It will be interesting to look back at these blockchain symbols and see which ones stood the test of time.

> Make art that you love and then figure out how to sell it. THANKYOUX, ARTIST

Generative Art Aesthetics = A Revival Generative art, made using a predetermined system that often includes an element of chance, has existed since the 1960s. The genre has exploded over the last two decades as a result of the open source movement, faster processing power, and a supportive community. AI art is a subgenre of generative art. Long-form generative art has been made possible and nurtured by the decentralized web. Furthermore, it is going through a revival thanks to developments in blockchain technology. Ecosystems ripe for collaboration and decentralization are the new frontiers for generative art today.

Art and Gaming Most of the behaviors that are surfacing in the Crypto Art movement come from the world of gaming. The medium of video games is post-contemporary art, and it is evolving quicker than other art forms as technology and societal views evolve; yet, not all games and NFTs merit the term of art or high art. But, to be fair, there are also terrible paintings and books out there, too. Most of the artists currently succeeding in NFTs are those who have made visuals for video games and other types of motion graphics. Video-game artists understand the power of communicating directly with their own communities; this is a

> Dedicate yourself to developing your own unique voice over the long term, and don't get caught up trying to chase short-term hype cycles. SARAH ZUCKER, ARTIST

new characteristic of the Crypto Art movement. Up until now, art was always a one-on-one psychological experience between the viewer and the art. Now, as a natural consequence of Web2 and social media, the Crypto Art movement is based on communities. Children of the 1990s and 2000s who spent their childhoods playing video games understand digital currencies, digital environments and the importance of buying online assets.

> **Have an answer ready: why does your art need to move into the NFT space? Know your crypto art history and where you fall into the context.** KAT COHEN, THE KRILLEST

How, then, can crypto art pieces make the transition from being loathed to being admired? Typically, museums have the last say on what constitutes art history. For an artwork to be accepted into a museum, it must align with the institution's mission, vision, and collections expansion strategy. When a museum acquires an artwork, it accepts permanent ownership for the item, ensuring the artist's place in history. The curators of a museum will investigate the market (galleries and artist studios) for works that fulfill the institution's aims and then present a selection to the board, who will then make a purchase decision.

Digital art and NFTs need time to mature. Museums are not innovators; by design, they are retrospective. Analyzing the influence of movements takes time, and digital art is no exception. However, the process has already begun. Most institutions are experimenting but not from a curatorial new artist perspective. Some museums, such as the Hermitage, are taking objects of our cultural patrimony, for example, masterpieces by Leonardo da Vinci, and are minting them as NFTs, mainly to register and protect the collection but also to raise funds for the institutions. If humanity were to move to Mars, we might have to leave the da Vincis but we would surely take the blockchain.

> **It's Art that you need to prioritize; the hype over forms come and go. Focus on the story that your artwork tells, and not whether you can profit from the NFT sale** GIZEM SAKA, PROFESSOR

NFTs under criticism

● 2.3 ● ●
It's bad for the environment

Artists have always drawn attention to the effects—both good and bad—that developing technology has had on the environment. In the 19th century, the Impressionists were known for their paintings of trains and landscapes changed forever by the new age of industry. In the early 20th century, photographers captured the rising of metropolitan skylines and the increasingly mechanized bustle in the streets below. In this current century, concepts of climate change and carbon footprint are at the forefronts of many artists' minds, and the advent of NFTs has brought art into a potential collision course with these concerns.

> Just do what you know how to do, and work from your heart. If it's sincere it will read. THE HAAS BROTHERS, ARTIST

The production of NFT art seems at odds with environmental protection because the blockchain technology that underpins NFTs relies on significant computing power to operate. The blockchains that support Bitcoin and Ethereum both use the "proof of work" (PoW) model, where participants in a peer-to-peer network are rewarded for "mining"—performing difficult mathematical computations to validate transactions. Whereas mining could initially be carried out on a basic gaming PC, the PoW system is designed to increase the complexity of the problems that require solving as more machines are added to the network. The increase in computer power (and, thus, the energy required to solve increasingly difficult computations) is a design feature of the system—the increasing energy requirement gives the blockchain increased protection against malicious use.

> Show up consistently and authentically, it's not about timing the market, it's all about time in the market. ALEJANDRO NAVIA, NFT NOW PODCAST

Mining an NFT uses a minimum of 142 kWh of energy, about the same energy needed for 100,000 credit card transactions or the daily energy use of five typical American families. The creation of just one NFT, versus the energy to power five American homes for a day. And purchasing and selling an NFT creates additional transactions that need to be validated, and such "mining" requires even more energy.

So, are NFTs all environmentally unfriendly, end of story? The answer is no. A new system for verifying and encrypting blockchains has emerged. Unlike the PoW model, which requires all computers in the network to validate each transaction and compete to be the winner, the "proof of stake" (PoS) consensus model requires participants to stake a specified amount of their currency as a guarantee that they will not act fraudulently. The network then randomly selects the computer that will carry out the validation, and that participant will be compensated for an accurate validation (or lose their stake if the network detects fraud).

> Calling someone an NFT artist is like calling someone a streaming musician. The NFT is not what sells – it's simply a tool. It's about your direct relationship to your fans and collective stewardship of your IP – and winning together. Stay away from the hype and focus on your art and how tech can take it to the next level. Art first, always. SWAN SIT, ENTREPRENEUR

In a nutshell, the PoS model is more energy-efficient. It eliminates the energy expenditure of the PoW model, where every computer competes to solve a problem but there is only one winner. The greener PoS model is the way of the future. Ethereum is heading that way, and when it has fully transitioned, its environmental footprint is predicted to reduce by an incredible 99 percent. Solana, Polygon and many other blockchains are already based on PoS. Artists and investors who are serious about environmental impact must do their business on PoS-based blockchains.

● 2.4 ● ●

It's only for the crypto bros

Artists of color, female artists and members of the LGBTQ+ community have been historically underrepresented in the traditional art market. A white male artist will sell more works, for higher prices, in more exhibitions than his less-represented colleagues, and he will have less of a challenge obtaining gallery representation. The system is decidedly undemocratic and arbitrary and appears to be run by an elite who are, primarily, white male painters. Just one comparison out of many possible examples demonstrates the problem very well: when Jenny Saville's *Propped* sold for $12.4 million in 2018, it became the most expensive piece of art by a living female artist; Jeff Koons's *Rabbit* sold for $91 million.

> Take everything you know about traditional art and disregard it. The ethos is that of an authentic community with a collaborative spirit. Granting creative access to other artists and collectors will benefit you tremendously. ASHLEY RAMOS, NIFTY GATEWAY

So far, so similar, in the NFT space. The Metaverse may be hailed as welcoming to all, but "crypto bros" (or "Degens")—white men—dominate the scene. The top ten NFT artists are almost all male; Grimes is the only female artist known to have made it into that list. And the share of the spoils is skewed dramatically toward male artists. Female artists account for 5 percent of NFT revenues, whereas approximately two-thirds goes to men (the remainder being uncategorized).

NFT projects exhibit a corresponding lack of diversity. In a world where scarcity and rarity are supposed to be factors that drive value, the example of Crypto Punks suggests otherwise: out of a collection of 10,000 Crypto Punks, 3,840 are female; yet, male Crypto Punks are often the most expensive. Analysis with respect to race is a more difficult proposition, as many projects do not include race or skin color as aspects of their items and there is a wide range of avatars (human, animal, alien). However, there is an underlying anecdotal suggestion that lighter skin tones may be linked to higher prices for the "human" NFTs. Even Beeple's $69.3 million NFT was not immune to criticism regarding diversity: after some observers leveled accusations of homophobia, racism and sexism in connection with the artwork, the artist responded with an apology and an affirmation of his liberal values and support for diversity and inclusion.

Similar to the traditional art market, the "winner takes all" mindset is prevalent in the NFT industry. Data from the platform Nifty Gateway shows that half of all sales were generated by only 16 artists. The top 25 percent of artists account for over 90 percent of the entire value. And they are mostly white, male Americans.

> The NFT space allows for artists to develop relationships with their buyers and fans that have previously been owned by intermediaries. Communicating with your fans and also contributing to the communities of the artists you collect provide such great opportunities to grow.
> JENNI THOMPSON, UNICORN DAO

Geographically, the market has three main epicenters: the United States, the United Kingdom, and Canada. More than 70 percent of all NFT sales occur in those three markets.

- → 174 US artists earned approximately 50 percent of all sales.
- → 40 UK artists earned 13.1 percent.
- → 15 Canadian artists earned 1.5 percent.

Although it is possible that Nifty Gateway's results may skew toward North America, their analysis shows that fewer than 5 percent of NFT artists come from Africa or Latin America. And, just as in the traditional art market, Los Angeles, New York and London are the leading centers: 51 artists in Los Angeles sold $35.2 million of NFT art; 50 New York artists sold $31.5 million; and 22 London artists sold $24.8 million. This analysis provides more than a mere suggestion of lack of diversity.

> Open up to different digital practices and understand how to use the blockchain to enhance your practice and learn, for instance, about programmable, generative and recombinant art.
> LUISA AUSENDA, ARTIST

It's not all negative, though. Granted, while white males from the millennial and Gen Z demographics may have had most of the fun (and business) up until now, there has been a noticeable shift in attitudes, with more artists working in collectives and collaborating. For example, joint ventures across genders and races have accounted for 20 percent of Nifty Gateway's revenues to date. Approximately a quarter of NFT purchases now come out of such

NFTs under criticism

initiatives, and this appears to be the current trend for artists working in a wide range of sectors beyond "art for art's sake"—sectors such as design, music, technology, athletics and entertainment.

Find your tribe, meet other artists in the space, support them by showing up and collecting their work when you can and spend 24 hours per day on Twitter. JUSTIN MELILLO, MONA GALLERY

Yes, NFTs have been a thing since 2014, but they are still a new concept. And, as with any new phenomenon, those with greater resources to invest will benefit early on. However, the nature of NFTs allows a more even playing field and improved access for early adopters regardless of how they may have been viewed by the traditional art world. There is great potential for underrepresented members of society to engage with the exciting new art world of NFTs and for that participation to contribute toward addressing socio-economic imbalances and diversity hurdles.

●Data Studies - Research Findings
●●●

Data Studies - Research Findings

● Participants in the traditional art market know surprisingly little about their markets. Many don't have information about market value, volume, average price points or recent trends because most such data is not available to them.

Web3 is going to change all this. It will now be difficult not to know what once was hidden. This chapter provides an overview of NFT art market data. ●●

●3.1●●
Art Market Data

When looking at data in the art world, two main areas can be separated out: NFT-related data and art market data. While art market data includes all transactions related to the global art trade (all art genres, time periods and mediums), NFT data is rather broad as it includes data from the financial, entertainment, sports and other industries. We will narrow this down to make it easier for you.

NFT data

The total value of sales of NFTs across all industries—not just art—is $17.7 billion for the full 2021 year and roughly $8 billion for the first quarter of 2022 (Source: Nonfungible.com). There has been an incredible quantum leap, given that in 2019 the total sales value was only $24.5 million. And also the number of NFTs sold has seen a dramatic increase: In 2019, 1.6 million NFTs were sold;

> Think about how you can extend the experience of art into the different dimensions in which humans experience reality. MELTEM DEMIRORS, COINSHARES

Data Studies - Research Findings

compare that to 27.4 million in 2021—and 7.5 million already in the first quarter of 2022! The number of participants has skyrocketed, as well, from 25,000 sellers and 45,000 buyers in 2019 to 1.2 million sellers and 2.3 million buyers in 2021.

Those numbers are impressive. Lots of NFTs bought and sold, and lots of people buying and selling them. Don't forget, though, that these numbers are for all categories—art, collectibles, metaverse, gaming, sports, utilities and more. For our purposes in this book, the two categories of most interest are art and collectibles, which are difficult to differentiate.

> Hard work and persistence is an important part of most successful artists' stories. Take the steps to plant the seeds and, after a while, you'll find yourself in a beautiful garden. JEN STARK, ARTIST

Artistic NFTs Artistic (or art) NFTs are created either directly by artists or by generative art algorithms coded by artists. You could compare this to the traditional art market: many unique artworks or smaller edition sizes. The focus is on the art, not on "utilities" (additional services). Examples of art NFTs are those created by Jen Stark and Hackatao.
Value: $1.6 billion • Transactions: 0.8 million

Collectibles Collectibles often come into the market in collections of 10,000. They can take the form of any type of digital object (e.g., profile pictures [PFPs], animals, planets and avatars), and they often come with utilities. For example, ownership of a collectible may allow its use in a video game or access to a restricted community. Bored Ape Yacht Club and Crypto Punks are two examples of NFT collectibles.
Value: $9.5 billion • Transactions: 4.6 million

NFT Art-related data

Artistic and collectible NFTs have seen a rapid increase in popularity and value. In 2019, less than 20 percent of the sales value of NFTs were art-related. Within the space of two years, their popularity and value went stratospheric: by 2021, sales of artistic and collectible NFTs constituted 63 percent of the total NFT market ($11.1 billion).

Of the two, artistic NFTs, which are the focus of this book, are the little sister. Collectibles dominated the market and were responsible for 85 percent of all art-related NFT transactions in 2021 and, by far, the larger share of the value ($9.5 billion for collectible NFTs vs. $1.6 billion for artistic NFTs).

> The internet is another garden in which to grow. Digital ownership of your work helps sow the seeds of your community. Coordination allows it to blossom. All those beautiful flowers create more demand for your work. It's the same old gardening except with new tools for the shed. SAM SCHOONOVER, COACHELLA

As it's the focus of this book, let us take a closer look at the number of buyers of artistic NFTs. Naturally, there has been a corresponding massive increase in the number of buyers. In 2019, approximately 1,370 buyers and 865 sellers were engaging with art NFT platforms. Two years later, the artistic NFT landscape had changed almost beyond recognition. In 2021, there were:

→ 84,182 sellers, including 43 percent active in primary sales (i.e., first-time sales of an artistic NFT direct to buyer) and 86 percent active in both primary and secondary sales. (The secondary market, or auction market, refers to when NFTs change hands a second time or more.)
→ 130,696 buyers, 64 percent of whom were active in primary sales and 76 percent of whom were involved in both primary and secondary trading.

And the 2021 numbers for the NFT collectibles market were simply next-level: 199,381 sellers selling to 484,226 buyers.

Average prices are always a good indicator to understand where the market is going. In 2021, artistic NFTs experienced a tenfold increase in average price, increasing from $300 to over $3,000. The average prices were $1,462 on the primary market and $5,485 on the secondary market. Collectible NFTs came in lower: $586 in primary sales and $3,108 in secondary sales. In 2021, the primary market accounted for about 60 percent of the volume of sales but just 25 percent of the value.

> It's not about the latest NFT drop, or even the utilities. The community that Web3 can build is the most important takeaway. Every artist has the potential to tap into either an existing community or cultivate and grow a new base. There's power in the people. AMANDA FAIREY, OBEY GIANT

Data Studies - Research Findings

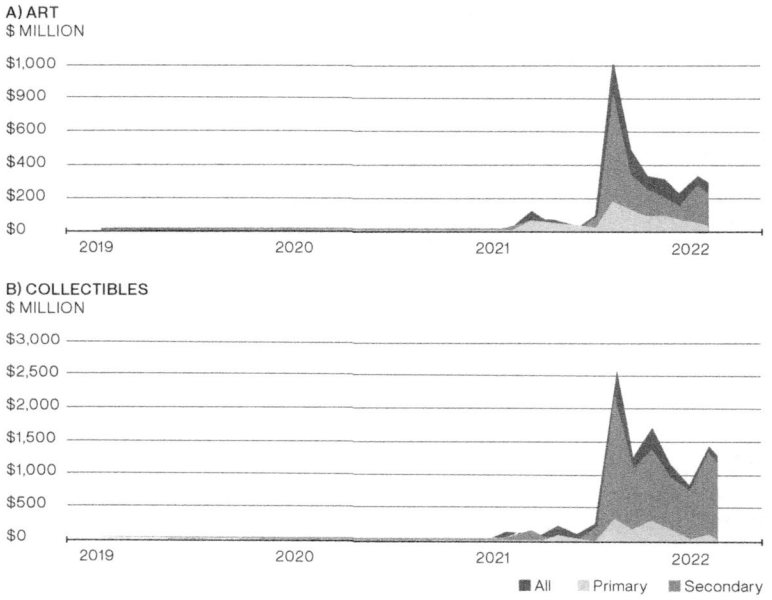

Monthly Values Traded In Art and Collectibles NFTs 2019–2022

Sources: McAndrew (2022), NonFungible.com (2022)

Downturn Following record highs in 2021, the market saw volatility in the first quarter of 2022. The crisis in Ukraine, government announcements to reduce "anti-Covid" financial assistance, increasing interest rates, and Tesla's plan to cease taking cryptocurrencies triggered this downturn. As a result, the cryptocurrency market has sustained massive losses, with $500 billion being wiped away. The NFT market is among the first to bear this enormous impact. It seems as if NFTs are taking a break.

> Do it for the art. HACKATAO, ARTIST

Overall, many indicators are bearish in Q1 2022:

→ There are fewer active buyers, as speculators are scared of losing money.
→ The number of transactions, the dollar amount traded and liquidity all declined. For example, the collectible NFT of Twitter co-founder Jack Dorsey's first tweet was auctioned for $2.9 million in March 2021. Early in

2022, the purchaser wanted to auction off the NFT. He did not accept the final offer, as it was lower than $14,000.

→ Primary market sales and volume are heavily impacted, more so than the secondary market. It seems that the primary market is not able to absorb huge volumes of new NFT projects. It's not surprising that the bulk of their value remains in the secondary market, which represents over 10 times the dollar volume of the primary market.

However, there are also some positive signs. Average prices have risen during the first quarter of 2022, which means that those NFTs that remain in circulation are acknowledged as being valuable. And, despite the fact that the number of active wallets is also falling, the number of buyers is still more than the number of sellers, indicating that there is still demand for NFTs.

While it is true that billions of dollars have been lost off the value of cryptocurrencies, with approximately $6.5 billion exchanged in the first quarter of 2022 for artistic and collectible NFTs compared to $11.1 billion in all of 2021, it cannot be said that the market for art-related NFTs has collapsed.

Traditional art market data

Contrary to the astronomical rise of trading activity in the NFT space, traditional art hasn't seen such a rapid increase in years. There are approximately 20,000 galleries, 1,500 auction houses, and 100,000 artists and art advisors involved in the buying and selling of around 40 million pieces of art every year. While these numbers may sound big—and the estimated annual value of the global art market as of 2022 lies somewhere between $40 billion and $65 billion (depending on which report you read)—it's not actually very large. For context, FedEx's 2021 revenue was $84 billion, meaning that a single player in the competitive logistics market pulls in more revenue than the entire conventional art industry worldwide.

> Think of the community and the way you engage with them as an art. RAJ GOKAL, SOLANA

Data Studies - Research Findings

Furthermore, the traditional art market is not showing any signs of growth. The numbers show a fairly stable plateau of $60 billion in annual sales. Similarly, the number of items sold (i.e., market volume) has held stable over recent years. The market is not thriving. Those at the top may be, but the rest of the market is in dire straits.

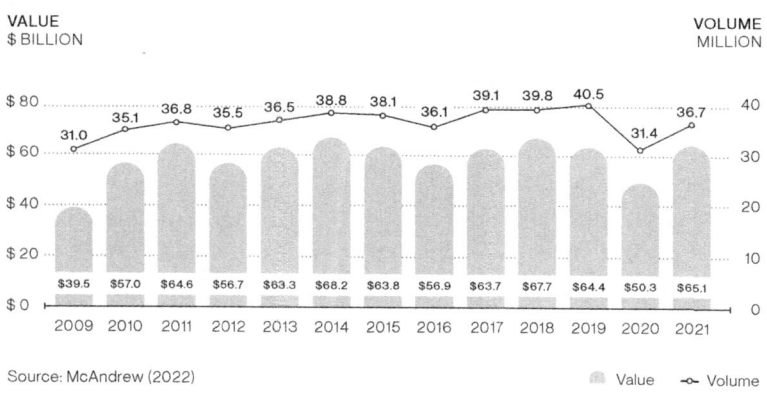

Sales in the Global Art Market 2009–2021

Source: McAndrew (2022)

The traditional art world did not join the party when it came to embracing the quantum change that internet trading has brought to 21st-century commerce. Only 20 percent of worldwide art sales are transacted online, a very small percentage when compared to other physical businesses that have undergone major transformations to reap the benefits of the internet revolution. Although the internet sites of galleries and other art players flourished during Covid-19—before the pandemic, only 10 percent of the market was online—there is not expected to be another significant permanent shift to online commerce. Buyers of traditional art remain fierce in their commitment to galleries and to purchasing their art the old-fashioned way. Online transactions in the traditional art world, when they do occur, tend to be limited to artworks with price tags less than $5,000.

> Enter with humility - think about why you're here and what you're adding before you consider how to extract value.
> LESLEY SILVERMAN, UNITED TALENT AGENCY

Comparing Market Data

To give the size of the NFT art market further context, let's compare it to the traditional art market. At $11.1 billion in sales value in 2021, the NFT art and collectible market began to rival the online art market ($13.3 billion) and represented about one-fifth of the total art market ($65.1 billion)[1]. The NFT market lags traditional art in terms of volume (5.4 million works sold vs. 36.7 million). The number of buyers is also significantly greater in the traditional art market. While we do not have a precise number, we estimate it to be more than 10 million compared to 600,000 NFT art and collectible buyers.

> Building a digital identity will open doors you didn't know existed, so use your own taste to create/collect what feels true to you, and you'll find your "tribe"—consistently explore, connect, and build with them, and watch what unfolds before you.
> CLAIRE SILVER, ARTIST

Interestingly, average prices are similar in the NFT and traditional art markets. The primary market average prices are under $2,000; in the secondary market, the average prices of collectibles and traditional art are higher, at around the $3,500 mark, and the average price of an art NFT is $5,500.

	VALUE	VOLUME	BUYERS	AVERAGE PRICE		SHARE	
				Primary Market	Secondary Market	Primary Market	Secondary Market
ART NFTs	$1.5 B	0.8 M	0.1 M	$1,462	$5,485	27%	73%
COLLECTIBLE NFTS	$9.5 B	4.6 M	0.5 M	$586	$3,108	27%	73%
TRADITIONAL ART	$65.1 B	36.7 M	10 M+	$1,873	$3,788	53%	47%

Sources: McAndrew (2022), NonFungible.com (2022)

[1] NFT sales are taking place on NFT platforms, and hence are not included in the $65.1 billion figure for the total value of the traditional art market.

Data Studies - Research Findings

What intrigues us is the flourishing resale (secondary) market, which has speculators moving in and out of NFTs at a considerably faster rate than is feasible in the traditional art market. In 2020, 75 percent of overall art NFT values and 79 percent of transactions were tied to primary sales. In 2021, however, the relationship between the primary and secondary markets experienced a dramatic reversal, with resales accounting for 73 percent of the value of trading in art-related NFTs. The traditional art market is more balanced: in 2021, the global primary–secondary percentage split was 53:47. In 2018 and 2019, gallery sales outperformed auctions in terms of sales growth, revealing a considerable divergence in the performance of the primary and secondary sectors over the past three years.

> As an artist, ask yourself: does this artwork need to exist as an NFT? Does it leverage the capabilities of technology in a way that enriches the connection between the artist and the collector, and in a way that traditional art forms can't? If the answer is 'no' or 'not yet', work with a creative production partner that understands how to elevate your artistic vision with web3 innovations and help you target the right audience for your project - whether that is first-time NFT buyers or established digital-native collectors.
> AUDREY OU, TR LABS

Another emerging trend is that the buyers and sellers of traditional art are increasingly favoring private sales, that is, art trades that are not publicly visible. Private sales by auction houses rose in value by over a third. While the NFT market is all about transparency, at the higher end of the mature traditional art market, private deals seem to be preferred.

Consider also the time an art piece is kept before being resold in each market. The average duration between purchase and resale of an art NFT is just 33 days. Compare this to the average holding period of 25 to 30 years in the traditional art market. Keep this in mind when we discuss the motives of NFT buyers. Speculative purchasers interested mainly in purchasing and quick reselling appear to be attracted by the higher liquidity and easier sales mechanisms. In contrast to the traditional art market, there are fewer obstacles to acquiring and selling due to the anonymity of transactions.

● 3.2 ● ●

Market Overview

After comparing the traditional art world to the NFT space, we will now shine a spotlight on the market players and trading levels. Broadly speaking, the traditional and NFT art markets have two main participating groups, artists and collectors, who interact in two main markets. In economic terms, the artists create the supply and the collectors generate the demand and they interact on trading levels.

Trading Levels

Artists and collectors interact on two trading levels, which we briefly mentioned before: the primary and secondary markets.

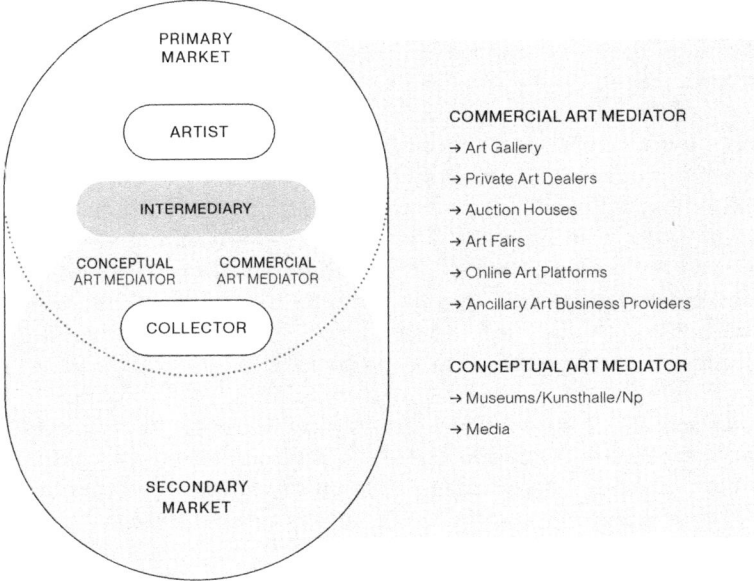

Source: Resch (2021)

Data Studies - Research Findings

Primary market The primary market deals with work that is being sold for the first time. The major stakeholders are working artists, galleries and buyers. There are more artists and purchasers, and the resulting competition often leads to cheaper prices than are seen in the secondary market.

Secondary market Most people think of the secondary market when they hear the term "art market." This is where art items are sold for the second time, and beyond. The sector is dominated by auction houses, established galleries and dealers in the traditional market, and by bigger marketplaces in the NFT space. Very few artists are involved in secondary market transactions.

> Think of an NFT as a medium. The more you learn the medium, the better the likelihood you'll create what you really want. QUHARRISON TERRY, ENTREPRENEUR

While both the NFT and traditional art spaces operate on these two trading levels, there are differences in the intermediaries that serve them. They can be divided into commercial art and conceptual art mediators. A commercial art mediator facilitates the exchange of artwork between an artist and a collector or serves as a reference for either party. Conceptual art mediators such as museums or the media participate in the transmission of information by communicating the message of art to a general audience. They exert a distinct but equally potent influence on the art market. There are fewer of these intermediaries in the NFT space.

Conceptual Art Mediators The role of conceptual art mediator in the NFT market is currently performed by the media, primarily by reporting record NFT prices and explaining the technological concepts. While it's true that there are some "museums of NFTs" and that some traditional art museums have accepted donated NFTs, there are very few such examples. This is important because museums and other non-profits play a crucial role in affirming value in the traditional art market. Their lack of support can have lasting implications on the manifestation of value of NFTs.

Commercial Art Mediators Commercial art mediators are equally important in the traditional art world. Galleries and auction houses are the main players, and they establish value—galleries, by networking with museums to exhibit their artists; auction houses, by recording public prices of artists. Whereas artists in the traditional space must participate in this networking (which will be explained later), this ecosystem is more or less irrelevant in the NFT space, as demonstrated by the sales numbers. Sotheby's and Christie's sold $230 million in NFTs in 2021 out of approximately $14 billion in overall sales. Polls of second-tier auction houses indicate that just 5 percent had traded in NFTs. And, according to a poll conducted by Artsy, galleries have adopted a similarly low-key approach to NFTs: in 2021, just 10 percent of galleries sold NFTs.

New commercial intermediaries have emerged in the NFT space in the form of the marketplaces where most NFTs are traded. Such marketplaces have assumed the functions of galleries and auction houses. Whereas online art markets such as Artsy will collaborate with galleries, NFT marketplaces bypass the galleries and collaborate directly with the artists under a new income-sharing plan. Compared to galleries that typically retain 50 percent, most NFT marketplaces retain less than 10 percent. And compared to conventional art auction houses that collect fees from buyers and sellers in the range of 10 to 20 percent from both parties, the NFT marketplaces collect just 5 to 10 percent on each transaction. In addition, the artist earns around 10 percent in royalties whenever their work changes hands; in the traditional art space, they earn zero.

Galleries

Galleries have been the most crucial commercial intermediaries in the traditional art industry, performing a gatekeeper role by introducing artists to the market and to museums and auction houses. The advent of NFTs has placed a question mark over their ongoing function and significance. What will their position be? Will they continue to perform a valuable function?

> Do something meaningful - it must make sense conceptually and aesthetically.
> JOHANN KOENIG, KOENIG GALERIE

The global gallery market for fine art is served by approximately 20,000 galleries in 3,500 cities in 120 countries. Europe and the United States are, by far, the most significant regions for the gallery sector, between them accounting for 83 percent of all galleries globally. Asia is still a very modest market, with just 9 percent of all galleries. As indicated earlier, galleries are hesitant about NFTs.

Data Studies - Research Findings

According to an Artsy report, 11 percent of galleries sold NFTs in 2021, 25 percent intended to include NFTs in their sales strategies in 2022, and 28 percent were uncertain. The galleries that sold NFTs in 2021 reported collector interest in the format, and almost 90 percent stated they would sell NFTs again in 2022.

The bigger the gallery, the lower the likelihood that it sells NFTs. To date, most galleries that have sold NFTs have been small, with less than five full-time employees. This suggests that the owners of smaller galleries are more inclined to experiment with selling new art forms and also that there is little interest from top collectors (who usually deal with larger galleries). Less than 10 NFTs were on display at Independent Art Fair 2022 or Frieze New York 2022, sending a clear signal that current interest from the traditional art world is tepid at best.

> The first question is what is the NFT space? It's not art. It's a way of monetizing and trading digital assets (and sometimes physical) through blockchain certification. My gallery artists focus on the art, not the certification. So my advice for artists is to focus on creating work that is unique and reflects what they want the world to experience. If adding an NFT to the work helps sell it, then so be it. But don't let the NFT dictate your creative output and how your work is defined. STEVEN SACKS, BITFORMS GALLERY

Nevertheless, there are some galleries that have exhibited digital art for longer than the current hype, for example, Postmasters, Bitforms, Transfer and Left Gallery (now closed). And other galleries have started more recently to experiment with NFTs, such as Stefan Simchowitz with Simco Drops, Unit Gallery in London with Institut.co, Koenig Gallery with Misa.art, Nagel Draxler who dedicated their entire Art Basel Miami Booth in 2021 to an NFT exhibition by Kenny Schachter, Kate Vass with her gallery in Zurich, and Adam Lindemann, who showed *Chromie Squiggles* by Snowfro in his New York gallery Venus over Manhattan in May 2022 and during Art Basel 2022.

Gallery participation in NFT sales is expected to increase. As mentioned, 25 percent of galleries surveyed by Artsy have signaled their intent to sell NFTs in 2022, a 150-percent increase over the number that sold them in 2021. There are other promising signs for artists. Although galleries have been slow to accept payment in cryptocurrency, that technology seems to have been accepted more readily than NFTs, suggesting that galleries are willing to interact with a new breed of collectors who are flush with crypto and keen to acquire art. Three leading art galleries, Pace, Gagosian and Lehmann Maupin, have stated that they accept cryptocurrency payments. Pace has built its own NFT platform (Pace Verso) and Gagosian hosted a show with his artist Takashi Murakami in collaboration with the NFT design studio RTFKT.

Given the attention that NFTs receive in mainstream media, it is surprising that so few jumped on the bandwagon to participate in it, offer NFTs and work with artists. From our conversations with gallerists, we often hear their resentment towards NFTs. This is partly due to the astronomic and unreasonable prices that some NFTs have achieved, the lack of context many projects have, some gallerists' resistance to being open to anything new, and the lack of access and understanding of a new technology. Just like artists, you cannot expect gallerists to welcome a new technology with open arms, given that this technology is not only difficult to understand but might also pose a risk to their existing business model. In all conversations, we have encouraged gallerists to embrace the change, and we hope that some will also read this book.

> Be prepared to connect with a new group of buyers - crypto natives. So run your own Discord and talk their language. JOE KENNEDY, UNIT LONDON

Collectors

After artists and commercial intermediaries, collectors play the next most essential role in the art market.

There are three types of buyers in the traditional art market: private buyers, corporations and public entities. Private buyers, mostly white men between the ages of 40 and 65, are the most active purchasers. Thirty percent of collectors are women, and that number is on the rise. The top three reasons cited by collectors for purchasing art are aesthetics (87%), passion for the arts (86%), and support for artists (79%). Between them, the United States and Europe are home to 83 percent of the world's art buyers—which explains why so many art galleries are located in those regions.

Data Studies - Research Findings

It is difficult to estimate the total number of art collectors. The group at the top—those who spend more than $100,000 per year on art—is rather small. We counted 3,000 buyers in this bracket who are collecting publicly. Assuming a similar number of collectors operating privately gives us an estimate of 6,000 big-spending art collectors, globally. This group is responsible for very few transactions, but the total value of those transactions is enormous. And then there are the "one-time buyers" who account for a large number of transactions but only a small share of the value.

Buyers of NFTs have different characteristics to buyers of traditional art. They are also mainly white and male but are younger than their counterparts (usually younger than 40). Their motivation to buy is primarily for financial gain rather than for aesthetic reasons. According to an ArtTactic report, 95 percent of those spending $25,000 on NFTs in the past 12 months cited investment returns as the key reason for their purchase. Similarly to traditional art buyers, they also value community and social reasons to buy NFTs, but those factors are secondary considerations for them.

> **It's a crowded space. You need to have a real vision for how to reach an audience.**
> ADAM LINDEMANN, COLLECTOR

Interestingly, men and women report different motivations for collecting NFTs. Whereas most men (95%) say they are interested only in financial gains, a far smaller proportion of female buyers (67%) purchase NFT art primarily for investment reasons. Compared to only 58 percent (58%) of men, a much higher percentage of women (76%) buy it because of their passion for art, particularly digital art.

As is the case for the traditional art market, the majority of value in the NFT space is held by a small number of purchasers. Chainalysis investigated all NFT transactions (not only art-related) between February 2021 and November 2021. According to their report, less than 10 percent of the 360,000 NFT owners controlled 80 percent of the market's value. So, roughly 40,000 individuals hold most of the total NFT value, which is comparable to the situation in the conventional art market. Regardless of whether you call them "whales" or "VIP collectors," both markets are dominated by elites, different groups that don't intersect much with each other.

3.3
Success Factors of NFT projects

The numbers have told us plenty about the NFT market and its players but they don't tell us why some NFT projects succeed while others fail. A closer look at some data studies may provide us with answers to that question.

Success factors in the traditional art world

First things first. Before we look at success research for NFTs, let's first consider the success factors for the entire art market. In 2018, Magnus and his team published a seminal paper exploring the factors contributing to the success of artists, based on an analysis of data from the traditional art market. Over three years, the team analyzed the careers of over 500,000 artists, considering over 10 million data points. The paper, "Quantifying reputation and success in art," represented a breakthrough in art market research, and the results were published in over 100 newspapers around the world.

> Stay true to your practice, remain honest and remember that digital has many paths to enhance your work. PAULINE FOESSEL, ARTPOOL

The research uncovered a data-rich map of museums and galleries and their respective influences on an artist's career. They were organized into networks by grouping galleries and institutions that exhibited the same artists. One hub was immediately noticeable and was given the moniker "the Holy Land." The hub includes the Museum of Modern Art (MoMA), the Guggenheim, the Metropolitan Museum of Art, the Art Institute of Chicago, and the Whitney Museum of American Art, as well as commercial intermediaries such as Gagosian, Pace, Hauser & Wirth, and David Zwirner. An artist exhibiting in the Holy Land is assured of gaining notoriety and high prices. The Holy Land offers artistic validation in its purest form.

Data Studies - Research Findings

The map also showed that there is only one route to success. If an artist is not part of the Holy Land, then they are stuck in an island network with all the associated limitations, and it is unlikely they will ever achieve success in the art world. Most artists who begin their careers outside of the Holy Land never rise, but most artists who begin their careers in Holy Land institutions remain at the top. The research showed that an artist's first five to ten shows were the most crucial for their career and that if an artist got discovered by a prominent gallery early on, their likelihood of achieving elite status was high. Conversely, if the first five shows don't include an exhibition at one of the top-ranked institutions, it is likely the artist will never be invited to exhibit at such a place.

> Employ Web3 technologies to bring your most loyal supporters together into a community who can dream, build and benefit together. Convert your audience into a crew and make the most of the power of the collective. BRIAN MARK, DAPPER COLLECTIVES

The discovery of this map and its implications was disheartening. Ninety-nine percent of all institutions scored poorly, exclusion from the central hub confined most artists to an island network indefinitely, and less than 240 artists who started showing on an "island" were permitted to access the Holy Land. When this research was presented to artists, they all asked the same question: "How can I reach the Holy Land?" How can one achieve success when quality is subjective and the market is demonstrably unjust and undemocratic? To answer these questions, Magnus launched an online class covering this topic. In a few hours of video lectures, www.magnusclass.com presents methods for finding art stardom. It's the go-to class for those who want to make it in the art world.

Success factors in the NFT world

In late 2021, Albert-László Barabási, a co-author of "Quantifying reputation and success in art," set out to apply the framework to the NFT market. His research analyzed data from Foundation.art, a marketplace for NFT art. Foundation is an open platform, allowing any active artist or collector to invite new artists. The goal of the study was to identify the factors that make some NFT artists more successful than others, and it employed a similar methodology as was used in "Quantifying reputation." A secondary goal was to determine if networks are as important in the NFT space as they are in the traditional art market. The findings of the study are as follows:

Few artworks sell The study extracted data for all NFTs on the Foundation platform up until June 2021. There were 50,723 works, of which 48,059 (94.7%) were listed for sale and 15,279 (31.7%) were sold. Of the NFTs that had been sold, 1,928 (12.61%) were re-listed on the platform and 138 were resold.

The numbers tell the story: 30 percent of listed items were sold; 4 percent of all offered works made it into the secondary market (i.e., they were sold again); and only 0.2 percent were sold three times. This shows how few pieces actually sell and then how few of them make it into the resale market. While the corresponding statistics are even worse for traditional art, the low conversion rates for NFTs are still striking.

> **Contribute more to the community than just the art you are trying to sell and show.**
> JUSTIN AVERSANO, ARTIST

Be a first mover Artists and collectors who joined early have benefited from first-mover advantages. Let's take a closer look.

The study classifies the adoption of new technologies into four temporal stages:

→ Initial Adopters: this corresponds to the first 2.5 percent of artists and collectors who joined the platform (from 21 January 2021 to 22 February 2021);
→ (2) Early Majority: represented by the next 13.5 percent (23 February to 10 March);
→ (3) Majority: 68 percent (11 March to 18 May);
→ (4) Laggards: the final 16 percent (19 May to 18 June).

Data Studies - Research Findings

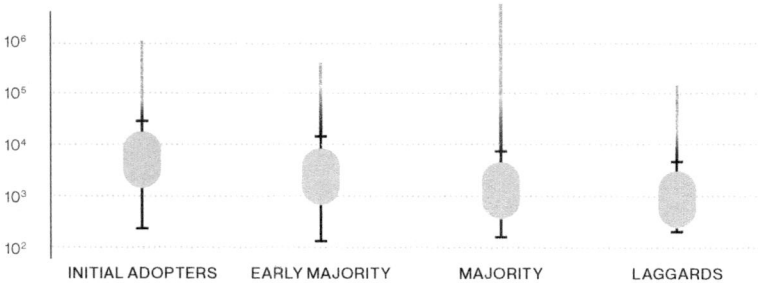

Source: Vasan et al. (2022)

The graph shows the earnings for the artists in each of the groups representing the four stages. There is a noticeable trend from higher total earnings for Initial Adopters down to the lowest total earnings for the Laggard group.

Barabási's study also revealed that NFTs uploaded by Initial Adopters sold at higher rates than works uploaded in the later stages. Seventy percent of the art released during the Initial Adopter period found a buyer compared to less than 15 percent of the art released during the Laggard period.

Choose your social media wisely Artists always want to know if the number of their followers on Twitter will determine their success in selling NFTs. Does the size of one's Instagram or Twitter following matter? The paper identifies a correlation between the number of Twitter followers and the success of an artist—but it's a weak one. However, the number of followers on the Foundation platform has a stronger, more direct correlation to the success of an artist. The number of Foundation followers is strongly predictive of how well an artist will do. Thus, having a large social media following elsewhere is not enough if it doesn't convert into followers on the platform. That means that artists must choose their social media wisely.

> **Verity over verification. Be true to your North Star and don't let the noise and hype overwhelm you.** ANIKO BERMAN, LEVELS AGENCY

Network is key Just as in the traditional art market, networks are vital in the NFT space. Artist networks provide this function instead of galleries and museums. To be able to sell on Foundation, an artist must be invited by a member already on the platform. The research suggests that the artist who does the inviting is a strong predictor of success, the implication being that if a person is invited by a successful artist they will likely be successful, as well.

> Artists have a beautiful way of seeing the world on their own terms and sharing that vision with an audience. This is a special time for artists to bring their unique perspective and leverage blockchain technology for their art, as their art, and as the medium for social commentary.
> MICHELLE ABBS, WEB3 EQUITY

Two groups were identified, and are referred to as "rich clusters" and "poor clusters." The rich cluster comprises artists who sell art for high prices. The poor cluster describes artists who sell their works at modest prices. When a member invites fellow artists to join Foundation, they are likely to invite acquaintances from the same category. In other words, a new member's success will often be comparable to that of the member who invited them. Therefore, it has become crucial for artists in the NFT space to think in terms of networks of artists. Who are the successful NFT artists? Connect with them, and benefit from the network effect.

Not convinced? Successful artists like Justin Aversano have begun to recognize and harness the power of their networks. Aversano's NFT marketplace, Quantum Art, invites unknown artists to exhibit, and these artists sell out because of the strength of his network.

Price history matters Because prices can fluctuate quite dramatically, the NFT space always tends to appear unstable. However, if we look deeper, that's not the case. For each artist, there is a range of prices within which their work moves, and that range is very stable. Barabási's study identifies three main price ranges. Works by artists in the top range sell for more than $20,000. Those in the middle price range sell pieces for between $1,000 and $20,000. The lowest price range is below $1,000. The study suggests that it is very unlikely for artists to move out of their ranges. Thus, an artist in the lower price range will typically stay there, selling items for several hundred dollars. A $100,000 sale would be highly unlikely.

Data Studies - Research Findings

Artists starting their careers who fear settling into the lowest price range must break into the higher ranges quickly. This could be done by limiting supply or focusing all collector interest on one or two sales to push up the work into a different price range.

> Making NFTs, I ask myself one simple question: does this work push forward (or challenge) the idea or audience of NFTs? If you make work that does, you will be found. You have an opportunity to contribute to a new art history, seize it.
> BEN GENTILLI, ROBERT ALICE

Keep a few powerful collectors close As the crypto art space lacks the formal roles played by commercial and non-commercial mediators such as galleries, curators and museums, success in this space is mediated by the artist–collector relationship. Instead of attracting a large number of new collectors, the success of NFT artists is contingent on their capacity to establish relationships with collectors willing to continue buying their work. That is, successful artists need only a few collectors who buy repeatedly and at high prices. Unsuccessful artists fail to build a consistent collector base, resulting in low-priced purchases from several collectors. Strong artist–collector relationships are prized in the NFT sphere, much as they are in the traditional art industry, where the most influential purchasers are known as Superstar VIP collectors. In the NFT space, they are called Whales.

The findings of the study can be summarized as follows. In the traditional art world, success is predicted by the network to which you belong. Join a top gallery early in your career and you will remain successful. In the NFT space, a different type of network is predictive of success: the network with fellow artists and collectors. The network with artists is important because the success of one artist spills over to that of another. The network with collectors is important because only a few collectors are extremely powerful in the NFT space. Such collectors buy actively and in depth; that is, they purchase many works by the same artist. Interestingly, timing matters

> Take your time, ask questions, experiment. You have a beautiful career ahead of you.
> SHANTELL MARTIN, ARTIST

in the NFT world, too. The earlier an artist joins a platform, the higher their prices will be and the more likely their works will sell. Finally, the number of Twitter followers an artist has is much less predictive of success than the size of the community that follows them on an NFT platform.

●Mint an
NFT●●●

Mint an NFT

● Ready to launch an NFT project? Anyone can mint their first NFT. There's nothing to be afraid of. We will run you through the necessary steps to get started.

And even if you aren't planning to launch a project publicly just yet, we encourage you to step through it with us. So, take out your laptop, and let's go. ●●

● 4.1 ● ●
What you need to get started

Most artists who work in the traditional art market wonder if they can sell their works as NFTs, given that they are not tech-savvy or they produce physical works, not digital files, and their works don't involve avatars or other digitally native subjects. When we are approached by artists who are hesitant about joining the Web3 movement, we respond without hesitating: Yes, you should experiment with NFTs. NFTs are here to stay and, since the technology is still in its infancy, now is the perfect time to explore how it might benefit your work.

> Ethereum is the world's next global settlement layer. Don't bet against it by minting your NFTs in any other ecosystem. RAHILLA ZAFAR, MINTED

You don't need a deep knowledge of crypto to mint—that is, to create—an NFT, but you do need a set of tools to get started. It takes only a couple of minutes to get everything set up. Here are the three things you need:

→ A digital wallet in which to store cryptocurrency and NFTs;
→ An account at an exchange platform to convert dollars into cryptocurrency;

Mint an NFT

→ Cryptocurrency in the wallet to pay minting fees.

Do not fear asking questions; everything in this space is ever-evolving, and asking for help should be encouraged! AMBER VITTORIA, ARTIST

The following instructions take you through the steps required to line up a wallet, fill it with crypto, and connect it to an NFT marketplace.

●4.2●●
Step by Step: Minting an NFT on a marketplace

● **Step 1: Set up an Ethereum Wallet** A digital wallet is where you keep the cryptocurrency needed to create, sell and trade NFTs. The wallet also has a secure facility that allows you to log in and create accounts on NFT markets in a similar manner to how Facebook logins provide secure access to Web2 platforms. Therefore, a wallet is a key component for Web3 activities. The sites listed below provide free digital wallets that should be compatible with most of the significant NFT marketplaces and blockchain applications. If you have trouble creating an account with any of these wallets, check out YouTube. There are hundreds of videos to select from that will run you through the exact steps on how to sign up.

Coinbase Wallet With over 90 million customers, Coinbase is the biggest cryptocurrency exchange, and its wallet may be a good choice for people who are new to virtual currency.

MetaMask The MetaMask cryptocurrency wallet is used by over 30 million crypto enthusiasts. The wallet integrates seamlessly with most crypto applications and NFT markets, and is available as a browser extension and mobile app for iOS and Android. With a MetaMask wallet, you do not need an account at an exchange platform to purchase cryptocurrency..

> 98% of successful artists have struggled for years, if not decades, to get to where they are. Prepare for the long haul and find joy in the journey. TREVOR JONES, ARTIST

Rainbow The Rainbow wallet is popular because of its beautiful design. Rainbow makes purchasing Ethereum on iOS as simple as using Apple Pay.

A word on safety. There are two types of wallets. Custodial wallets (or hosted wallets) are controlled by an exchange and are accessed using a login and password. The wallets listed above are all non-custodial wallets, meaning they are self-managed. We recommend them because

Mint an NFT

non-custodial wallets give you full control and do not depend on a third party to keep your cryptocurrency secure. When you register, you will get private keys, a seed phrase (12 to 24 words) that gives you access to your private key, and public keys.

Think of it like this: If your wallet were a bank account, the public key would correspond to your account number, while the private key and seed phrase would represent your PIN. Just like an account number, the public key is what you share with others to allow transactions to occur. And, just like a PIN, you must not share the details of the private key with anyone. If you forget those details, you will lose access to your wallet. Moreover, if a third party were to learn them, they would have complete access to your assets.

- **Step 2: Purchase cryptocurrencies** Once you've opened a wallet, you'll need to add some currencies to it, since in most marketplaces there are costs associated with converting your files into an NFT. Of the many cryptocurrencies available for purchase, Ethereum (ETH) is the one most commonly used by NFT platforms. We suggest you purchase about $50 worth of ETH.

Let yourself get gutted over and over again. RACHEL ROSSIN, ARTIST

Both Rainbow and MetaMask wallets enable you to purchase cryptocurrency from inside the wallets using a credit card. Coinbase Wallet requires you to convert dollars to cryptocurrency on an exchange platform before transferring them to the wallet. Coinbase, Kraken, and Binance are three well-known exchange platforms.

- **Step 3: Choose a marketplace** Your choice of NFT marketplace may affect whether or not your NFT artwork sells. It's not enough to choose where to sell your work based on the fees you'll pay; you must also examine which one of the NFT marketplaces best matches the NFT you are making and which blockchain the marketplace employs. In the NFT space, marketplaces have taken on the role of galleries. If you exhibit your work at Gagosian, it's more likely to be sold than at a less-established gallery.

We've compiled a list of the top NFT marketplaces where you can mint and sell NFTs. One of these should meet your requirements, whether you're buying, selling, or just interested in NFTs. Even if you're not planning to utilize an NFT marketplace immediately, now is a good time to learn what they are and how they function. For those of you just getting started with NFTs, we propose minting your first work on OpenSea because the site has the simplest and most straightforward setup.

> Have patience, think long term, and don't optimize for quick cash. If you think it's short term, it won't work. DMITRI CHERNIAK, ARTIST

Although you don't have to restrict yourself to a single marketplace, we suggest you concentrate on one or two channels. Collectors will want to locate your art. By minting and presenting your work on one marketplace (such as OpenSea), you will not only increase your chances with the platform's algorithm but you will also experience an increase in organic traffic, as people will know where to find you.

- **Step 4: Connect your wallet to the Marketplace** When your wallet has been set up and you have purchased some ETH, select the marketplace where you would like to mint and list your NFT and list your work. If you choose OpenSea, hit "Create" in the top right corner of the screen and connect your wallet. As you will see, connecting the wallet is similar to a Facebook login. A window will prompt you to enter your password. And, voila, you are connected!

- **Step 5: Uploading the file you want to turn into an NFT** So now you have a wallet containing ETH and connected to a marketplace. Find the area to upload a file. The file formats that are usually accepted are PNG, JPG, TXT, GIF, WEBP, MP4 and MP3. You will most likely be given three options:

→ Single (a unique piece, often referred to as a "1/1").
→ Edition (a series of the same work, often limited, sometimes "open," which means unlimited).
→ Collection (a series of similar works that each have their own properties).

For every artist releasing a new NFT, we recommend scarcity above unlimited supply. At best, you want your project to be completely sold out, giving collectors the impression that they have something that others covet but cannot have. If you begin with a collection of several thousand items, you are unlikely to sell them all. Therefore, keep your NFT runs small, with a few unique pieces—perhaps an edition of around 10 or 20.

Mint an NFT

A collection of 1,000 items or more should be considered only if there is an existing community prepared to buy from you.

- **Step 6: Setting up an auction for your NFT** In the next part of the form, you'll be asked to define the elements of your offering.

  Time Period The time period defines when buyers can place bids. There are usually three options:

→ Fixed Price / Buy Now: allows you to set a price and sell your NFT instantly.
→ Unlimited Auction: People can continue placing bids until you accept one.
→ Timed Auction: an auction with a time limit.

There are further options that can be selected for auctions:

→ Silent auction: Each participant declares anonymously the price they are willing to pay for the item. At the end of the specified time, the work is purchased by the highest bidder. This approach is used more commonly in the traditional art market than with NFTs.
→ Dutch auction: The asset's selling price decreases incrementally over a certain time period, and the sale is made to the first bidder. In some instances, the seller will set a reserve price. The deal is terminated if the selling price reaches the reserve price without a bid having been received. While they are not so common in the traditional art market, Dutch auctions have become fairly popular in the NFT space, as buyers enjoy the gamification aspect.
→ English auction: This is a "typical" auction, where the price is progressively increased with each higher bid. If the reserve price has been met and there are no more bidders after a set amount of time, the auction will conclude with a sale to the highest bidder.
→ Bonding Curve: This is a more complex auction but one with a simple logic: The more NFTs that are sold, the more expensive they get. So, early buyers will pay less than the last buyers. The formula for bonding curves is rather tricky, as you don't want your NFTs to become so expensive that nobody can afford them anymore.

> Take one idea and do it well. Stay true to the idea and to yourself. Good design is key, which means leadership has to maintain the big picture. Forget messy roadmaps – it is difficult enough to execute one concept. SENECA, ARTIST

Set the Price The most difficult part of the process is determining the price of your NFT (or, occasionally, the minimum price). If your price is too low, the transaction costs may erode your profit and put you in the red. As it is such an important decision, we have dedicated a section below to discuss pricing in more detail.

Additional features Beyond ownership of the art that is represented by the NFT, it can also be sold with additional features, often referred to as utilities. For instance, the NFT might allow the purchaser to visit your studio or bring VIP tickets to your next opening, or it might entitle them to a physical copy of your work for free. You can enter the details of such utilities in the "Additional Features" section. We will discuss utilities extensively in a section below.

> Translating your work into different mediums always teaches you about new techniques, ideas and frameworks, just try it out! KENNEDY YANKO, ARTIST

Royalties Royalties are fundamental to the NFT market and are a key point of difference from the traditional art market, where the creator does not benefit directly from an increase in the value of their work once they have sold it. So, if your buyer sells the work a few years later for ten times the initial price, you won't see any of that. This changes with NFTs. Artists who sell NFTs will continue to receive royalties from all future sales regardless of how many times the NFT changes hands. Thus, artists will now be able to benefit from an increase in the value of their work. Royalties are automated, so there is no risk of payments being misallocated.

A royalty plan is provided as an opt-in feature on platforms such as OpenSea and Rarible, allowing you to specify royalty payments. Every month, the platforms will send you any royalties collected. Determining the exact figure is a balancing act. Whereas a greater percentage may earn you more money per sale in the long run, it may also discourage people from buying your work in the first place since they will be less likely to make a profit. In most cases, we suggest you specify a 10 percent royalty.

> Do a stunt. AMANDA CASSATT, SEROTONIN, MOJITO

Properties If you are offering a collection, you have the option of adding your file's properties. For example, similarly to how Bored Apes does it, you could list the unique characteristics of a particular piece that differentiate it from the others in the collection. (If you don't have a larger collection or edition—we recommend that everyone start small—the "Properties" feature is irrelevant.)

- **Step 7: Adding a description to sell your NFT** The title and description of an NFT listing are very significant. Many artists are not used to penning lengthy descriptions of themselves and their works. However, considering the unfamiliarity of the audience with the work (and with the artist and their past work), a description is vital. It should be brief and succinct and written in common language.

- **Step 8: Paying the fees** The final step in minting an NFT is to click "Create Item." Some marketplaces (such as OpenSea) don't charge for minting NFTs; others (such as Rarible) do. Before paying, a word of warning. There can be four levels of fees in a marketplace:

→ Listing fee (kept by the platform): This is the fee, typically around 2.5 percent, to list an NFT on a platform.
→ Gas fee (not kept by the platform): Blockchains charge NFT platforms a fee for minting, buying and selling. A useful analogy for gas fees is the role that highways play on a road trip. Some highways are free to use; others charge tolls, which can be cheap or expensive. Some tolls will vary depending on the current traffic. If a large number of people are trying to mint NFTs at the same time, costs will be higher. We have seen minting (gas) fees of up to $100. However, most platforms have changed to a cheaper solution and costs will now be more in the $1 to $30 range. Some platforms waive the minting fee for creators, minting the NFT only once a buyer has finalized their purchase. Thus, the buyer will pay the gas fee as part of their purchase. Artists prefer this approach, as it minimizes their upfront costs, but there is a risk that a high gas fee will deter a buyer from finalizing their purchase.

> The art comes first – then persevere, and never give up. KENNY SCHACHTER, ARTIST

→ Commission fee: If someone buys your NFT, you'll have to pay a commission fee on the sale. These are usually in the range of 2.5 to 5 percent—nothing compared to the 50-percent gallery cut that is the industry standard in the traditional art market.
→ Escrow fee: You will also need to pay an escrow fee (sometimes called a transaction fee) to transfer the money from the buyer's wallet to yours.

●4.3●●
Marketplaces

NFT markets are essential to the sale of NFTs. As discussed previously, they take on the role of art galleries, curators and art consultants. The signaling effect of selling on a carefully selected platform is comparable to that of exhibiting at a superstar gallery. In addition, some markets are quite specialized, offering editions only, while others function only on certain blockchains. The majority of digital artists are active on several marketplaces, as the platforms don't usually demand exclusivity.

> Genuinely try to join the community. People can tell if you're trying to extract value rather than add to the collective experience. JOHN CAIN, SUPERRARE

Generally, no tech skills are necessary for minting, and as described above, iminting is free and a relatively straightforward operation. In contrast to the conventional art business, artists can anticipate receiving over 90 percent of the sale price after paying marketplace fees such as listing, gas and commission. And, in addition to that 90 percent, artists can look forward to receiving 5–10 percent in royalties when their works are resold.

The following is a list of NFT markets, with brief descriptions.

Opensea - The eBay of NFTs

NFT TYPE
ART, MUSIC, SPORTS, PHOTOGRAPHY, COLLECTIBLES, GAMING, AND MORE.

BLOCKCHAIN
ETHEREUM, POLYGON, SOLANA, KLAYTN.

FEES
GAS FEE, COMMISSION FEE OF 2.5 PERCENT OF EVERY TRANSACTION (EITHER BY BUYER OR SELLER).

PROS
↗ COVERS A BROAD RANGE OF NFTS.
↗ ACCEPTS OVER 200 CRYPTO-CURRENCIES.

CONS
↘ USES MAINLY ETHEREUM, WHICH STILL HAS HIGH GAS FEES AND A BAD ENVIRONMENTAL FOOTPRINT (NOTE: RECENTLY ADDED SOLANA, SO THIS WILL REDUCE GAS FEES.)
↘ SINCE LISTING IS FREE, THERE ARE A LOT OF FAKES ON THE PLATFORM.

Mint an NFT

OpenSea is comparable to eBay in Web2; it is a clearinghouse for practically all NFTs and collectibles such as video games, software and digital artworks. It is the largest market for digital products. Rob Gronkowski's GRONK Championship Collection (Gronkowski was the first professional athlete to mint NFTs) and Kings Of Leon's most recent album, one of the first major records released as an NFT, are among the items available on OpenSea.

> Be curious, connect with other creators and listen to what they have learnt. Most of all, make a start, jump in with an open mind and prepare for a whole new perspective. HOLLY WOOD, RARIBLE

Artists can mint on the blockchain at no cost and without the need to write a single word of code. OpenSea is the most democratic and user-friendly platform available. Anyone can establish an account and begin minting NFTs with no kind of verification required.

Rarible - Like OpenSea, but more expensive

NFT TYPE
ART, GAMES, PHOTOGRAPHY.

BLOCKCHAIN
ETHEREUM, FLOW, TEZOS.

FEES
GAS FEE, COMMISSION FEE OF 2.5 PERCENT OF EVERY TRANSACTION (EITHER BY BUYER OR SELLER)

PROS
↗ CHOOSE FROM SEVERAL BLOCKCHAINS.
↗ COMMUNITY-OWNED THROUGH DAO STRUCTURE (SEE BELOW).
↗ CAN OFFER LOW CARBON AND GAS FEES.

CONS
↘ RISK OF BEING DOMINATED BY BIG BRANDS.

Rarible is comparable to Opensea in that it is democratic and accessible; anybody can mint an NFT. People can purchase and trade NFTs in several areas including art, photography, games, metaverses, music, domains and memes.

While Rarible allows every user to create and sell their own art NFTs, there are two options when it comes to minting. As is the case for OpenSea, you can choose to mint for free. If you enable free minting, the buyer of your NFT will cover the fees. However, free minting adds your creation to the Rarible collection (collections are like folders for NFTs), not your own. To launch your own collection, you have to cover the minting fees. That's why we generally advise you to pay the minting fees. What sets Rarible apart from other platforms is its decentralized autonomous organization (DAO). We explain DAOs in detail below, but for now, briefly, the advantage of DAOs is that users can participate in governance decisions through a voting mechanism. Meaning that, rather than just being a customer of the platform, a member also has a say in the running of it.

SuperRare - The art gallery

NFT TYPE
DIGITAL ART.

BLOCKCHAIN
ETHEREUM.

FEES
GAS FEES, COMMISSION FEE OF 15 PERCENT OF EVERY TRANSACTION (BY SELLER), COMMISSION FEE OF 3 PERCENT OF EVERY TRANSACTION (BY BUYER).

PROS
↗ UNIQUE, CURATED ARTWORK.
↗ GOOD CONTENT AND AN EDITORIAL BLOG.
↗ AN OFFLINE LOCATION (GALLERY SPACE) IN NEW YORK CITY.

CONS
↘ ACCEPTS VERY FEW APPLICANTS.
↘ EXPENSIVE.

SuperRare, founded in 2017 and one of the "older" platforms in the industry, is one of the top NFT marketplaces for artists. Unlike Opensea and Rarible, it has a significant emphasis on rare, single-edition digital artworks and is strictly curated. Therefore, it only works with a small group of artists. It imparts a gallery-like atmosphere to the NFT area, prioritizing creative legitimacy and aesthetics over meme-friendly or celebrity NFTs. Only one percent of artists that apply are admitted, which may seem elitist (and counter to the ethos of the blockchain), but it means that artists who are chosen will have their work included in a collection of well-selected and highly curated artworks. SuperRare is similar to Rarible in that it is also organized as a DAO.

> **Learn by emulating the best, but don't just copy and paste. The community rewards innovation and will pay a premium to those that push the space forward in a new way.** MATTHEW LIU, STORY.XYZ

Mint an NFT

Foundation - The artist community

NFT TYPE
FINE ART, PHOTOGRAPHY, DIGITAL ART, 3D ART.

BLOCKCHAIN
ETHEREUM.

FEES
GAS FEE, COMMISSION FEE OF 5 PERCENT OF EVERY TRANSACTION (BY SELLER).

PROS
↗ CURATED AND LIMITED NFTS.
↗ A MARKETPLACE FOR ARTISTS, BY ARTISTS.

CONS
↘ DIFFICULT TO GET INTO.
↘ EXPENSIVE.

Foundation is like an exclusive artists' club. It is a community-curated platform administered by a small group of artists. To join Foundation, you must receive an invitation from a current member, and each member can send only one invitation.

Nifty Gateway - The Harrods of NFT marketplaces

NFT TYPE
VERIFIED AND CURATED ART DROPS.

BLOCKCHAIN
ETHEREUM.

FEES
GAS FEE, COMMISSION FEE OF 5 PERCENT OF EVERY TRANSACTION PLUS $0.30 (BY SELLER).

PROS
↗ PAYMENT BY CREDIT CARD IS POSSIBLE.
↗ TRUSTED AND STRONG BRAND DUE TO GEMINI BACKING.

CONS
↘ A FOCUS ON CELEBRITY NFTS.

Highly curated, Nifty Gateway is perhaps the most difficult marketplace for artists to sell on. It is owned by Gemini, a blockchain business founded by the Winklevoss brothers, who came to prominence when Mark Zuckerberg paid a $65 million settlement relating to the creation of Facebook. Nifty Gateway has teamed with prominent artists and singers such as Grimes and Beeple

> The medium is unexplored and expansive for visionary artists. All of the artists in history books arrived at a similar frontier and defined their legacies; that challenge is now in front of you. KAYVON TEHRANIAN, FOUNDATION

to issue collections of edition NFTs.

Nifty Gateway is the only major NFT site that accepts credit cards, setting it apart from every other platform on this list. The art on Nifty is typically expensive, almost as expensive as the art on SuperRare.

Build a community. DUNCAN COCK FOSTER, NIFTY GATEWAY

MakersPlace - The art world partner

NFT TYPE
COMMERCIAL AND FINE ART.

BLOCKCHAIN
ETHEREUM.

FEES
GAS FEE, COMMISSION FEE OF 15 PERCENT OF EVERY TRANSACTION (BY SELLER).

PROS
↗ MOSTLY VERY ESTABLISHED ARTISTS (MANY FROM THE TRADITIONAL ART MARKET).
↗ RARE NFTS.
↗ EASY TO USE.

CONS
↘ OFTEN VERY EXPENSIVE.

MakersPlace is an exciting NFT art marketplace. Here, renowned galleries, artists like Damien Hirst or organizations like Christie's sell NFTs. In contrast to other markets, MakersPlace artists often sell limited quantities of unique editions, thus generating exclusivity.

Magic Eden - A Better OpenSea?

NFT TYPE
ART, PHOTOGRAPHY, COLLECTIBLES, GAMING AND MORE.

BLOCKCHAIN
SOLANA.

FEES
GAS FEE, COMMISSION FEE OF 2 PERCENT OF EVERY TRANSACTION.

PROS
↗ GAS FEES ONLY A FEW CENTS AS SOLANA IS A MORE EFFICIENT BLOCKCHAIN.
↗ LITTLE SPAM AS ACCOUNTS NEED TO BE VERIFIED.
↗ LAUNCHPAD FEATURES MAKES UPLOADING EASY.

CONS
↘ THE WEBSITE HAS HAD SOME DOWNTIMES OR CAN BE SLOW.

Mint an NFT

Magic Eden has evolved as a serious competitor to OpenSea. As it runs on the Solana blockchain, its users benefit from cheaper fees and faster transactions. Also, the interface is easy to use, making minting and trading easy for every artist, including those who don't know how to code.

Story.xyz - Shopify for Web3

NFT TYPE
ART, MUSIC, PHOTOGRAPHY, COLLECTIBLES, SPORTS, VIRTUAL WORLDS, AND MORE.

BLOCKCHAIN
ETHEREUM.

FEES
GAS FEE, COMMISSION FEE OF 7.5 PERCENT OF EVERY TRANSACTION.

PROS
↗ A NO-CODE "SHOPIFY" SOLUTION FOR EVERY CUSTOMER.
↗ CUSTOMIZATION IS POSSIBLE.
↗ MODIFIABLE SMART CONTRACTS.

CONS
↘ NO EXISTING AUDIENCE.

Think of Story.xyz as the Shopify or Squarespace of the NFT world. Story allows you to create your own website to sell your NFTs rather than uploading them to a marketplace where they can be found amongst many other projects. Story's pricing is comparable to other marketplaces and, hence, presents a real alternative if you would like to retain more control over your presentation. The website is easy to build and requires no coding experience.

Find the tools and platforms which will help you connect with like-minded people; NFTs are more about community than anything. The rest will come naturally. CIPHRD, FX HASH

Other marketplaces to take a look at are Objkt, FX Hash (for generative art), which both run on Tezos, a blockchain liked by many artists and which partnered with Art Basel in 2021 and 2022.

● 4.4 ● ●
Pricing your NFT

Pricing in the art world is not necessarily logical or rational, and it can be a challenge to determine an artwork's price. There are a number of factors that can affect price:

→ Materials used to make the work, and other related expenses.
→ Time spent on the production.
→ Size.
→ Motive.
→ Edition size.
→ Your résumé.
→ Who collects your work and whether it was part of a notable exhibition.

As we all know, none of these criteria really matter when it comes to pricing. A better way to find the right pricing is to look at what buyers are willing to spend. Here are a few numbers to guide you:

→ In the NFT world, around 75 percent of all purchases on OpenSea (the largest NFT marketplace) were sold for less than $500.
→ The average selling price of NFTs fluctuates frequently. Recently (June 2022), it has decreased to less than $2,000, compared to a record high of about $6,900 in January 2022.
→ Most online buyers in the traditional art market spend less than $5,000 annually.
→ In art galleries, the average price for a contemporary artwork in 2018 was $9,335. If you sell your work straight from the studio, buyers may expect it to be half the price that they are quoted by galleries.
→ Ninety-two percent of works sold at auction sell at prices below $50,000, and 70 percent sell for less than $5,000.

> Be third. No reason to be first. Wait a while and see how it shakes out. Understand the ecosystem. YORAM ROTH, CULTUREWORKS

We strongly suggest pricing your works at less than $1,000. There are two convincing arguments for this. First, $1,000 is more in accordance with the purchasing patterns of

Mint an NFT

existing consumers. Second, your biggest client category are customers who have never purchased before. Therefore, it seems prudent to price artworks toward the lower end.

> Artists of all mediums and levels of education and success should explore creating NFT art, as it enhances their practice, collector base, and provides them a new way to earn and save money.
> DAN MIKESELL, BLACKDOVE

Consider your pricing to be a marketing tool that must be consistent with your brand and target market. Don't make it too difficult for collectors to part with their cash; one of the primary reasons people don't purchase art is uncertainty about what to purchase and how much to pay for it. However, it is also true that higher prices may attract more affluent customers, and pricing your work too cheaply would send the impression that it is of low value. Additionally, from the NFT success study we discussed above we learned that for each artist, there is a price range within which they move. Also, keep in mind that you will benefit through royalties earned from any resales in the future, so you don't need to make all your money from the first sale.

Balancing this is not always simple, but experience will help. Generally, the greater the quantity of an artwork, the lower its value. For instance, a 1:1 will likely cost more than one out of an edition of 100 or one out of a collection of 1,000. Based on a thorough review of existing pricing structures and buyer spending power, we propose the following guideline:

SIZE	JUNIOR	SENIOR
1:1	$1,000	$3,000
EDITION OF 100	$200	$600
COLLECTION OF 1,000	$100	$300
OUTLIER	$50,000	$100,000

● 4.5 ● ●
Intellectual Property

A discussion of NFTs would be incomplete if it did not cover the topic of Intellectual Property (IP) law. This is because NFTs could potentially disrupt the way we currently think about IP in the art world. The process of minting an NFT allows any creative work, such as art, literature or music to be transformed into a digital asset that can be stored on a blockchain and put up for sale on host marketplaces. This process raises many questions: What am I allowed to mint? Is the buyer of my NFT now the copyright holder, and will they be allowed to do anything with it? What are smart contracts, anyway?

We've discussed resale royalties, tracking ownership and adding utilities to the NFT. These things are all governed by two central contracts:

→ Smart contract: The smart contract is a code-based blockchain component that automates things such as ownership, transfers, royalties and fees.
→ License agreement: The license agreement is a contract that records the transfer of the rights advertised by the artist or project.

Thus, whenever an NFT is minted, you automatically write these two contracts. They are called "smart" because, in contrast to traditional contracts, they are digital, they are stored on the blockchain, and they help parties reach an agreement without the need for a middleman such as a lawyer, notary, or any other entity.

> Take time to learn the technological aspects of NFTs. Don't alter your creativity to try and fit into this ecosystem; technology should only be a way to enhance an artist's work. MICAH JOHNSON, ARTIST

One of the most important aspects governed by these contracts is the issue of ownership of the NFT and content. It is a distinction that artists are familiar with. When an NFT (or any tangible artwork) is bought, the underlying intellectual property rights are not instantly acquired by the purchaser. Copyright stays with the creator, who has the sole right to reproduce, generate derivative works from, perform, and distribute the protected work. When a person

Mint an NFT

purchases a painting from an art gallery, they take possession of the painting, which they may display, but they don't have the right to copy, create derivative works, or use the artwork on their company's marketing reports. The same principles apply to NFTs. An NFT buyer does not obtain the legal right to take photographs of the artwork, create T-shirts or prints or use it on their reports unless the NFT creator has granted specific permission (through the smart contract).

> Making an artworld is a team sport. Let's build a better art world together. NATO THOMPSON, ARTWRLD

These are the current rules. However, in practice, once an artist uploads their work to the internet, it becomes incredibly difficult to retain control and monitor who is using it, and for what purpose. In many countries (for example, the United Kingdom), creators are not able to register copyright. This makes it difficult to verify ownership, curb infringements, or effectively commercialize works. Consequently, several NFT artists began experimenting with new copyright licensing systems. Bored Ape Yacht Club, a collection of 10,000 profile photographs and one of the most successful NFT initiatives, grants the owners of its NFTs exclusive permission to use the artwork in any way they want, including for limitless commercial usage, so long as they continue to possess the original NFT. This implies that the owner, not the creator, may monetise the NFT, for example, by putting it on catalogs and T-shirts or perhaps licensing it for a film. Dapper Labs, the operator of the well-known NBA Top Shot platform, has announced a template NFT License that permits the buyer of the NFT to not only show the image linked with the NFT but also to sell merchandise based on that artwork up to a maximum revenue of $100,000 each year.

> Be smarter than the smart contract. There is no magic. Understand fully the actual contractual agreements that inform it. NANNE DEKKING, ARTORY

Some artists invite their communities to help develop their creative stories. Historically, this sort of collaboration has occurred behind closed doors with a single author or team of writers sworn to secrecy via non-disclosure agreements. Artist Micah Johnson created 10 chapters of the story of "Aku" by allowing the buyers of his NTFs to participate in the creative process by helping decide character and story elements. Aku has now been optioned for TV and film. This was the first time that an NFT project had provided original content for Hollywood, sourced as it was by a Web3 community with a built-in audience. Jenkins the Valet, an avatar and book project, allowed NFT holders to vote on aspects such as the creative direction of the story, the book's title, genre, plot, ending, cover art and illustrations. Even more, the creators have signed with Creative Artists Agency (CAA) for representation in books, film, television, podcasts, and other media.

However, some NFT projects are tripped up by intellectual property problems. When Pablo Picasso's granddaughter Marina announced plans to mint the world's first Picasso NFTs, the rest of the family didn't approve, proclaiming that the NFTs would be counterfeits. And when Quentin Tarantino revealed plans to sell NFTs based on his original handwritten Pulp Fiction screenplay, Miramax, the company that produced the legendary 1994 picture, filed suit within days. Miramax accused Tarantino of contract violation, copyright infringement, and trademark infringement. At the time of writing this book, the conclusion of this lawsuit is impossible to predict but it will undoubtedly serve as a cautionary tale for future NFT endeavors.

> For each artist, there is a range of prices within which their work moves. And that range is very stable. JENKINS THE VALET BORED APE YACHT CLUB, TALLY LABS

There are several lessons to be learned so that you avoid running into the sorts of issues that foiled the plans of Marina Picasso and Tarantino:

→ You need to be the original creator of the work that you want to mint. You cannot use or create something that's closely inspired by someone else's work.
→ By default, NFTs follow the same IP laws as physical artworks. The copyright always remains with the creator.
→ Smart contracts allow for experimentation, such as inviting your audience to collaborate in your project or even passing on licensing rights.

Ultimately, the artist creating the NFT is fully responsible for ensuring they have obtained the necessary permissions. But once that is done, then they are in charge. Smart contracts and licensing agreements allow artists to interact in new ways with their audiences.

●4.6●● Fraud & Theft

Fraud and theft have always exerted their malign influences on the art market. It is no different in the NFT space, although here it is taken to a new extreme. Whereas in the traditional art market, fakers and fraudsters focus only on a few highly successful artists, in the NFT space, almost any artist can become a target and be subjected to hundreds, even thousands, of fake NFTs generated per day, fake works that get sold and resold. Therefore, despite the fact that more people than ever are joining the NFT and crypto market, caution is necessary, as well as education regarding the risks associated with NFTs. In this section, we examine the most prevalent NFT scams and provide advice on how creators and buyers of NFTs can best avoid them.

> Be careful to protect your intellectual property by reading the terms and conditions of the platform. When appropriate, register your copyright to protect against copycat/infringing uses by others. PAUL COSSU, LAWYER

- **Plagiarized NFTs and art theft** Digital artists whose artwork is hosted on websites such as ArtStation and DeviantArt are seeing their work being copied then sold as NFTs on blockchains. As it gets easier to mint NFTs, this form of theft is becoming an even larger concern. The surge in plagiarized NFTs is due to bots scraping artists' web galleries and then generating collections with automatically drafted texts, as can often be found on OpenSea. Why Opensea? Because as we described above, it permits "lazy minting," where minting fees don't have to be paid until an NFT sells. If an artist discovers a fraudulent NFT based on their work, they have to contact the website to file a complaint, which is then dealt with manually. Thus, the process from discovery to removal is time-consuming.

When purchasing an NFT, do your research. Verification of a seller's account on OpenSea is shown by a blue checkmark. Follow the seller on social media and investigate their past transactions on NFT markets. Also, check for complaints. If the artwork you are considering has been stolen, you will likely discover internet records of the true owners.

- **Untrustworthy sites and links** When you purchase an NFT, you are purchasing proof of ownership. One may access the artwork itself through a link. Frequently, artists upload their work to Google Drive, Dropbox, and other cloud storage services. The buyer may then visit the site to download the file. Solutions are being sought to solve the problem of separation between the asset and the smart contract; for instance, blockchains Solana and Avalanche are developing ways to store both the digital file (e.g., artwork, video, MP4) and the NFT metadata files in a single package, so that when you purchase the NFT, you can be certain that you also have the artwork.

Until that issue is resolved, you must be careful. When you purchase an NFT, save the digital file that represents that NFT to a secure location; do not just accept a URL that links to the digital file. Ensure you have it, and preferably save it offline (on a USB). Do not keep your NFT file in Dropbox or Google Drive.

- **Marketplaces can disappear** NFTs are still in the early stages of their development. Some platforms on which you currently rely may not exist in the future, or their ownership may change and support may cease. Such disruption could result in your submitted files getting lost. Protocol Labs' InterPlanetary File System (IPFS) provides a method for storing your artworks on the blockchain. It enables users to pin an NFT to their platform so that it remains accessible even if the original marketplace where it was issued ceases to function. However, IPFS retains only the metadata; therefore, NFTs that point to URLs may still be lost. Services provided by sites such as IPFS2Arweave.com will attach your NFT to the IPFS and store the data on the Arweave blockchain. There is no longer any need to worry about data loss—as long as Arweave continues to run. Thus, "IPFS + Arweave" is more a contingency plan than a complete solution.

> Think about how blockchain technology can further your practice, and be authentic in your approach. MICOL APRUZZESE, VERTICAL CRYPTO ART

- **The rug pull** "Rug pull" is the term used in the NFT space to describe a project that has been abandoned by the promoters after it has generated a large sum of money quickly via hype and bluster. The promoters take the money and leave the investors with useless NFTs.

Mint an NFT

One of the more egregious rug pulls featured an NFT that capitalized on the Bored Ape Yacht Club frenzy. Evolved Apes was a 10,000-piece NFT collection that claimed to finance a blockchain video game using the NFTs. After raising $2.7 million, the founder vanished, leaving NFT owners with nothing except JPEGs.

> Enter with caution and be realistic in your approach, knowing it is a long play. The Wild West days are done and it takes a team with long-term vision to execute all the moving parts of that rapidly evolving world. BRIAN CHAMBERS, CURATOR, WRITER

Through simple investigation, for example, examining the creators' social media profiles, examining their history on NFT markets, and tracing a project's connections, you may be less likely to be the victim of a rug pull. A strong development team will also include their experience and connections on LinkedIn. Solid NFT initiatives will have a thriving social media community well before any NFTs are issued or any money is exchanged. Be sure to examine engagement rather than followers and check for discrepancies; fraudsters often pay for followers but they can't fake interest.

- **Pump and dump schemes** The art world is notorious for bidding up prices, cornering a market in order to raise prices, or creating hype around certain artists by artificially driving up demand—a technique called "pumping and dumping." Sellers buy back their own NFTs under false names and accounts to increase prices. Once they have a high enough demand, they sell their NFTs and leave the market. Buyers are then left with overpriced items nobody wants to buy.

> If the marketing is insanely impressive, exciting and original, it can carry your entire career. SAMANTHA JAMES, SUPERDIGITAL

To avoid a pump and dump, a good starting point is to look into the histories of the wallets. Here you can see all sales and transactions undertaken by the buyers and sellers. When you see two wallets buying and selling frequently to each other, you should be suspicious. Check out EtherScan, where you can examine every transaction on the Ethereum blockchain, if you want to drill deeper. You can also check the engagement on a project's Discord or Twitter.

Here are a few pointers that may help you to verify projects and identify possible scammers:

- Check their social media

  → Engagement rate: Check the engagement rate (total engagement divided by total followers, multiplied by 100). If the percentage is less than 1, the account might be fraudulent.
  → Celebrity endorsements: Do they seem authentic? Does the celebrity promote other products, too?
  → Misspelled names: Scammers will often intentionally misspell the names of accounts, providing account names that, at first glance, appear to be authentic.
  → Verified accounts: Some marketplaces and social media platforms allow users to display a blue checkmark to show that the account is verified.

- Check their website

  → About us: Check who is part of the team. Do they have LinkedIn profiles and other social media presence?
  → Roadmaps: Many NFT projects promise to provide utility in the future and they illustrate their intentions with roadmaps. Read their documents to see if their plans make sense. Or are they just copied and pasted from other projects?
  → Unrealistic mint price: Every successful community started at an affordable level. If the start price is affordable, consider it. If the only conversation is around floor prices, that is, the minimum investment required to get in, then get out!

- Check Discord communication Discord is the communication platform that many NFT buyers and sellers use to communicate. Think of it as a big chat room, split up into different rooms and channels. Many artists who launch projects also open their own Discord channels and invite potential and existing buyers to join. The following are things to watch out for on Discord:

> Web3 presents wonderful opportunities for artists. DYOR and be sure to find your tribe. Community is everything. SIAN MORSON, COLLECTOR

  → FOMO culture: Discord moderators pressure others to invest quickly, using such tactics as saying that you might miss the opportunity if you wait.
  → Predatory tactics: Some members can be threatened by moderators and others may be banned for asking questions or listing their recently bought NFTs for cheaper prices than what they paid for.

Mint an NFT

- → Fake giveaways: Members of the Discord can be bombarded with too many free giveaways.
- → Bots: Bots are swamping Discord, Twitter and many marketplaces, and they're a big problem. You can identify bots on Discord by their odd speaking pattern that doesn't sound human.
- → Airdrops: Once you become active on Discord, your wallet will start receiving "airdrops," random artworks issued by artists you haven't communicated with. These are analogous to the flyers that you find in your mailbox.

● How to stay safe

- → Never connect your wallet to any random links.
- → Never share your seed phrase or password with anyone.
- → Write your seed phrase on a piece of paper and KEEP IT SAFE in a location you won't forget. If you forget and lose this seed phrase, you will not be able to access your wallet.
- → Do not click on links from unknown senders or those that could possibly be malicious.
- → Do not download unfamiliar apps or copy and paste unfamiliar code.
- → Do not scan QR codes from people you do not know or whose legitimacy you cannot verify.
- → Enable two-factor authentication to maximize the security of your account.
- → Always check the URL to make sure it's not a fake (misspelled) copy of the authentic site address.

●How to build a Web3 Community
●●●

● The most important pillar in any NFT project is community. Notice how many of the quotations from our experts refer to it. While the word "community" can be overused, we cannot stress it enough.

In this chapter, we will explain what we mean by it and discuss how to build a community. ●●

●5.1●●
The idea of a community - Basic concepts

Technology has always historically made its mark on society. We are currently moving out of Web2 and into Web3. As a reminder, in Web2, platforms monetize the content that we upload to them, and they own our creations and data. Think of Instagram and how they sell advertising space by using the images we upload to it. However, a transformation is underway. With Web3, it is no longer desirable to spend hours on social media in the hope of accumulating "likes" and followers. Users can now own their digital assets and monetize them. Ownership is the key component of Web3.

> A huge advantage of Web3 is the ability for creators and collectors to establish a direct relationship. Lean into this. Collectors want to know the individual behind the art, the inspiration behind their work, their personal successes and struggles. KEITH GROSSMAN, TIME

In this framework, creators and their communities support each other by owning the same digital assets together. The idea is that every participant holds a stake in the community's growth. This is easily seen with Bitcoin and Ethereum—both of which have seen cult-like communities develop around their tokens. While there is no tangible value attached to either of these communities, the sheer power of a community has an intangible value. If you join early, you are likely to feel more psychological reward than someone else who joins later and doesn't contribute as much to the project. This psychology is the superglue that keeps the community thriving, working and contributing toward growth. In this model, money moves in circles between all members of the community instead of in one direction from the platform to the creator. Translated to the art world, this means, for example, that the members of an engaged art lover community are rewarded for the time they spend supporting an artist.

Blockchain technology plays a substantial part in allowing this idea to unfold. No longer does one centralized platform control everything; rather, the community does, and it uses tokens to verify who belongs to it. Your support of an artist is demonstrated by your purchasing one of their NFTs. If you support a certain cryptocurrency, you own some of that currency. Thus, only by owning a currency such as Bitcoin are you part of that community. And you are rewarded when the price goes up. You can be similarly rewarded after purchasing an artist's NFT—if the artist has understood the power of their community.

> **Make a conscious effort to educate yourself on blockchain protocols and smart contracts. The more you understand the possibilities and implications of the technology, the better equipped you'll be to create and sell art in the space.** J.N SILVA, ARTIST

Like everything else in this movement, communities can be decentralized, permissionless and global. You don't need a contract to work for a community, and you don't need to be in a certain geographical location. All you need to do is participate and provide your skills together with other like-minded artists that are working toward the same goal.

Community vs. Audience

As you can see, we have been using the word "community" a lot. Many times, it is used to refer to an audience. However, audience and community are not the same thing. Your following on social media is not your community. A community is a close circle, a tightly knit and active group of people working toward the same goal.

Think about it. How many unpaid hours have we all spent on social media trying to promote our Instagram page, only for Instagram to profit? We do this with the sole purpose of getting people to look at our art and hear our message. What if there was a way to take our Web2 audiences and turn them into Web3 communities? This is the key to the future of creative labor and a thriving freelance economy that is abundant and passion-based.

> Persistency – keep on doing what you are doing and don't follow any trends.
> DAMJANSKI, ARTIST

Let's take a look at the differences between an audience and a community:

AUDIENCE	COMMUNITY
→ CONSUMERS AND FANS	→ LOYAL MEMBERS AND SUPPORTERS
→ LIKES, COMMENTS, DMs	→ VOTES, PARTICIPATION, EXCHANGE
→ ARTISTS AND FANS ACT INDEPENDENTLY FROM ONE ANOTHER	→ COLLABORATION BETWEEN MEMBERS AND ARTISTS
→ THE NUMBER OF FOLLOWERS MATTERS	→ ENGAGEMENT AND PARTICIPATION MATTER
→ ONE-WAY CONVERSATION (FAN TO ARTIST)	→ MULTI-WAY CONVERSATION (FAN TO FAN, FAN TO ARTIST, FAN TO ARTIST TO FAN)
→ DATA IS OWNED BY THE PLATFORM	→ DATA IS OWNED BY EVERYONE
→ NO REWARD FOR SUPPORT AND TIME	→ REWARDS FOR PARTICIPATION; "ENGAGE TO EARN"

Building a community is about building loyal members who are supportive of your idea. You can do this by giving them voting rights, allowing them to participate in your projects, and exchanging ideas, as well as assets, with them. In contrast, an audience just "likes" and follows you, but there is no participation. In Web3, participants can come up with initiatives that are in the spirit of the artistic community and the founders of the community can endorse it. The artist doesn't always have to act on every initiative. There is room for people to propose, create and mobilize. If the members of your community are interacting with each other in a true Web3 manner, then you could ask them about their background and what they are interested in, and they could even vote on future initiatives. You can create work around the data gathered.

Stay true and don't follow trends. Be active in the space, talk with people, listen to them, learn from them, be on Twitter and Discord. Things take time. Stay humble and thankful. DOT PIGEON, ARTIST

● 5.2 ● ●

Step by Step: Building a Community

At Rally.io, Tam saw many examples of thriving communities that grew organically using diverse strategies. Supportive people were committed to developing the utility of projects, shifting the focus from a transactional mindset ("What do I give and what will I get in return?" or "What does purchasing a coin immediately get me?") to a co-owner mindset, where they had an actual say and could participate in the direction of growth and enjoy continual rewards, access and opportunities that would increase exponentially as growth occurred. It's important to understand that artists selling on marketplaces are left on their own. The support system that a gallery offers is not available to help launch and market the art. Here are some steps that lead to success that we have observed by analyzing artists selling NFTs:

> NFTs are an opportunity for artists to form deeper connections with collectors and art/tech lovers alike. The technology is constantly evolving and this ever-shifting medium affords new creative possibilities. There is a global stage for NFTs and a growing audience for digital artwork. It's a new world with endless opportunities. JACLYN LAVY, SOTHEBY'S

● **Step 1: Define your purpose** Working toward something bigger than oneself will be the glue at the core of your community. Your community's purpose will sustain it over the long term, even if some members might fall off. Every good artist has a topic of research on which they base their work. Whether it be the environment, feminism, identity, justice or nature, a purpose like that is bigger than any one artist or collector or community member. A community that embraces the same purpose will be willing to build with the artist, and it will be sustained by that purpose.

The mission statement is a brief description of a company's core purpose. It answers the question, "Why does this business exist?" Ask yourself what your purpose is. Why are you creating art? Whom do you want to influence? Your mission statement should describe what you aim to do and why you are doing it. Sit down and write one for yourself. Keep it short. To give you an idea, let's look at some examples, including the original Microsoft mission statement, which, although long since updated, remains among the very best of its kind.

→ Microsoft "A computer on every desk and in every home."
→ Uber "We ignite opportunity by setting the world in motion."
→ Tesla "Tesla's mission is to accelerate the world's transition to sustainable energy."

● **Step 2: Identify your community** This is not an exact science, but the idea is to mobilize everyone you know around your message to become active contributors to a community. The first step is to define your community.

The natural community member for you is someone who can connect with the work you do and who loves it and, maybe, shares your personal values, lifestyle, or passion. Don't only include people who can afford your work, as you will also want to include those who are your supporters but don't yet have the means to acquire them. Visualize the life of your preferred member. Ask yourself:

> Simplicity is king. Don't over-engineer the project. Utility is not a must. In the end, it's about the art work. OXB1

→ What interests do they have?
→ What car do they drive?
→ Where do they live?
→ What clothes do they wear?
→ Where do they vacation?
→ What magazines and papers do they read?
→ Through what channels could that person be reached?

Again, think beyond just the top collectors and consider the potential of all those whom you have engaged with but are not (yet) part of your collector circle.

● **Step 3: Define roles in your community** In audiences, there are followers; in communities, there are leaders with roles. Activism is a great example of this because people are donating their time, energy and passion voluntarily for a cause. There is usually not just one leader but many leaders who organize efficiently and create roles for participants.

> NFTs can be more than JPEGs or MP4s. They can act as keys, programs, tickets, promises or secrets. They can unlock, reveal, evolve, be redeemed, be destroyed, be combined. There are so many possibilities. SKOT LEACH, COLLECTOR

Not everything needs to fall on the artist. Most artists just want to do their work in their studios. They don't want to be managing Discords, shooting content, posting on Instagram, editing videos and doing other marketing things. That is why people have roles in communities. The flexibility of Web3 communities is such that employment contracts or agreements are not required; the roles are flexible and fluid. You can engage people to help you with your art shows and assign them temporary volunteer roles, and you can incentivize them with digital assets.

- **Step 4: Create a desirable offer** When you are selling a NFT, don't just think of selling another art piece. Similarly to the traditional art world, successful NFT projects have used marketing features to promote their works. While this might sound new to some artists, remember that in the NFT space there are no galleries that help you create the offering plan, sell it and employ sales techniques. Below, we have identified these functions in more detail. We explain the meaning of utility, rarity, scarcity, desirability, liquidity and value.

- **Step 5: Start your marketing** Think of NFT projects as exhibitions that you are hosting in a gallery space. A press release on the day of the exhibition is never enough to market it. Marketing your project requires serious preparation, as you cannot rely on the marketplace to send you clients—customers of marketplaces, as well as traditional galleries, are not limitless, and supply usually exceeds demand. There are certain elements that successful NFT projects have established to successfully launch their NFT drops:

    90 days before launch Create a whitelist. NFT whitelists are reserved spots in private sales that guarantee collectors a limited number of mints while members of the public have to rush to buy the remaining supply designated for public sale. This is similar to the practice of "VIP Previews" in the traditional art world, where selected clients are offered works before the gallery or art fair opens the show to the public.

> Imagine a possible world and use art with an endemic crypto to instantiate it IRL. MICHAEL JOSH ROSENTHAL, BANKLESS

How to build a Web3 Community

15 days before public launch Issue a free NFT to potential ambassadors of your community. These are people who are leaders or key stakeholders in your community. Ideally, they will share the work and thereby excite the community about the upcoming launch. Before the public launch of his Avatar project, Micah Johnson airdropped Akutar mint passes to all his Aku chapter holders so that they could receive a free NFT before the public had access. They also announced that all the funds will go to building an ecosystem of film, TV, games, experiences and products called "The Akuverse," driving value back to the community.

> Be yourself. Be your community. MIKE DUDAS, 6TH MAN VENTURES

At launch A launch, the goal is to bring maximum attention to your project using a range of communication channels in addition to real-life events. We have seen several activities on launch day that work to create buzz:

→ Create immediate utility after purchase of the NFT, for example, by providing a free asset (airdrop) for everyone who purchased.
→ Publish a story about the launch in magazines, newspapers and blogs to get credibility.
→ Organize a physical event and showcase it on your social media channels.
→ Post to social media the results of your primary market sales, as well as early results from secondary market sales.

10 to 20 days after launch A few days into the project, it's time to show your community that you are truly inviting them to participate in the future of the project and allowing them to engage with each other and feel a personal stake in what you are doing. A good start would be to survey their needs and wants. What are their interests and skills? What are they looking for in this community and what can they contribute? Here are some questions you could ask:

> Everyone is clamoring for attention, and the outlets are oversaturated. Find out what makes you truly stand apart. Be remarkable. ALI SPAGNOLA, ARTIST

→ What is it about my art that has brought you into this community?
→ What perks of this token excite you most? (e.g., NFT drops, access to the artist, the opportunity to meet like-minded people or contributing to the community).
→ Do you have special skills or interests you'd like to share?

- → Are you interested in having an active role in this community?
- → Do you have any specific ideas for the community?

60 days after launch After you have collected the initial round of feedback and have received several proposals, it's time to engage your community further. Allow them to vote on three different proposals, for example, where your next exhibition should be or if you should invite them to a studio visit or guided tour at a gallery show.

A good example is the Doodles project, a collection of 10,000 NFTs. Owning a Doodle allows you to vote on things like community proposals, get access to live events and participate in funding new Doodle projects. This makes the project highly collaborative and engaging for the community

> Art in Web3 has become the canvas that has connected communities, putting artists in a prime position to become our leaders of the future. Now is the time to find your niche and build around it! CHRIS ADAMO, FLAMINGO CAPITAL

90 days after launch Utility, roadmaps and hype around the launch are all important steps toward a successful project. Now, as time passes, it's just as important to deliver on the promises you've made, as collectors have given you their money to build something. Many projects that have started with ambitious and comprehensive roadmaps can often run into organizational challenges and not be able to keep many of the promises they've made.

●5.3●●
Creating Your Offer

When an artist sells an NFT, it's not often just a single piece of art. The NFT concept allows you to sell different versions, each with modifications on the theme. You can attribute unique characteristics to each NFT in the offering. There are many ways in which the offering can be varied, and this is one of the reasons why NFTs have seen such success. Creators love the endless opportunities and variables available for them to work with. So, when designing your offer, it's no longer enough to create a piece of art and then ship it to a gallery that will then try to sell it. It's about engaging the available technologies and using them to your advantage.

> NFTs today are primarily about money and large numbers, I'm not interested in this. I'm interested in art and its cultural value. So don't create just NFTs. Create art and certify it on the blockchain. WOLF LIESER DAM, DAM GALLERY

Single vs. Editions vs. Collections

In the NFT space, many offerings are referred to as "projects" or "collections" because most NFTs are sold not as a single item but in the form of either editions or collections. As we have described above, there are three broad categories:

→ Single (a unique piece, often referred to as a "1:1").
→ Edition (a series of the same work, often a limited edition but sometimes offered as an "open edition," which means it is unlimited in number).
→ Collection (a series of similar works, each of which has unique properties).

While single NFTs and editions are very common in the conventional art world, particularly with prints or photography, collections are a new concept. It is common to see collections of 10,000 NFT pieces that can be used as avatars, PFPs or abstract generative art. The number is not fixed. It can vary from 1,000 to 20,000, or more, depending on the creator's view of the likely demand.

The difference between collections and editions is that collections have rarity. This concept was developed out of the traits that characterized the NFTs in the CryptoPunks collection. An artist develops a collection by generating items with distinctly different characteristics that are defined using digital picture layers that are readily altered. Examples of features include clothes, backdrops, hair, colors, facial expressions, eyes and accessories. The layers are automatically integrated by software to create the collection. Rarity in collections is useful because it drives the value of the offering. It also produces excitement and creates a sense of self-expression and personalization for community members. It is considered best practice to limit these rare traits to one percent of the quantity of NFTs in a project. Thus, if your project has 1,000 NFTs then only 10 of them should possess rare traits.

Features of an NFT drop

NFTs can take various forms and come with a multitude of optional features. Here are some ideas to consider:

Desirability When rapper Post Malone, DJ Steve Aoki and television host Jimmy Fallon—and many others —changed their Twitter profile pictures into Bored Ape Yacht Club (BAYC) characters, many of their fans also wanted to buy a BAYC character and become part of the same "exclusive" club of BAYC NFT owners. Just like owning a Warhol or Rothko, ownership of an NFT can be a form of self-expression and provide proof that you are part of a movement. Thus, the NFT is rapidly becoming a new form of cultural currency. NFT owners will often show off their NFTs as status symbols by displaying them as profile pictures—a practice known as "flexing." And as the Medicis exerted a significant influence over the business of art

> You must consider how brand collaborations will benefit you, your community and the brand, as well as its consumers. Ensure that all collaborations feel meaningful and authentic for people; establish your limits but still be flexible. ELAV HORWITZ, MCCANN WORLDGROUP

and politics in the Renaissance period, today's "crypto whales" support, promote and influence the success of NFT artists and projects whose values align with their philosophy of decentralization.

Urgency An artist can also use FOMO to their advantage. In the conventional art world, urgency is created through auctions, VIP events that give pre-access to events and lists that are distributed to collectors before official launches of shows.

> Stay true to who you are and unleash your creativity. Imagine your story without physical limitations and take advantage of a full sensory experience and tech, immersing collectors in narrative, emotion and an ongoing experience. JASMINE MAIETTA, ROUND21

Urgency is used frequently in the NFT space, often in the form of whitelists or allowlists which are similar to VIP lists in that being "whitelisted" means that you get access before the general public. For example, when Zona Maco, Mexico's leading art fair, launched their first NFT collection, the NFTs included access to private tours of artists' studios as an extra utility. When marketing the collection, they set a deadline for purchasing the NFTs.

Scarcity Scarcity is a key marketing tool in any business. When there is only a limited amount available of something that is desirable, its value will rise. Given that NFT's are digital products, scarcity is a factor in every project. For example, when he launched VeeFriends, GaryVee capped the number of NFTs at 10,255. The number itself was not important, but what was important was that he limited availability to create scarcity.

Value A collector obtains value on many different levels by buying an artwork. The purchased piece can fulfill the buyer's aesthetic desires; the art may fill (perfectly) the white space on the wall above the sofa;

> You're one tweet, one share or one artwork away from success—stay at it. FEYYAZ ALINGAN, BLUE ALPINE RESEARCH

ownership may signal to others that the owner belongs to a desirable social class; or the art may be purely an investment that is expected to appreciate in value. As we have seen, the current motivations to buy NFTs are mostly financial in nature. There are many examples of collectors who have made fortunes buying NFTs.

While it is true that in today's NFT market, most community members care more about floor prices than the artist—or even the art—we believe that that is a characteristic of an unhealthy community. A healthy community will talk about the story, the art and the sustainability of a project, and most collectors will have "diamond hands," meaning they will sell eventually but are holding on for the long term. NFTs can be good investments not only when they sell on the secondary market but also if they catch the interest of traditional content production companies, as this could lead to publishing opportunities (e.g., books, podcasts, films and TV).

Liquidity Liquidity has historically been a major challenge for the art market. If there are no buyers, you can't sell. You can buy an artwork from a gallery for $10,000 and the next day find nobody willing to buy it from you, not even for $1,000. At least there is more liquidity in the secondary market; however, as discussed earlier, most works never make it there. In the NFT space, it's very similar, but some projects see more demand than supply, thereby creating liquidity. Although it's hard for artists to create highly liquid markets for their work, consider liquidity when deciding on the size of your collection.

> **Focus on building a community instead of profits. The digital space does not replace physical art; it's a complementary tool.** ZELIKA GARCIA, ZSONA MACO

●5.4●●
Keeping Your Community Engaged

Once people have purchased your offer and a community has developed, keeping them engaged is the next fundamental challenge. In the traditional art world, collectors will receive infrequent updates via email from the gallery that is showing the artist. And, usually every second year, past buyers will receive notification that the artist has been granted a solo show to display new works. Web3 technology enables new ways to keep your community engaged, via tokens. There are three main types of tokens:

> Be patient. It took me 5 years to get where I am now. SNOWFRO, ARTIST

- → Utility tokens: Utility tokens were developed for use inside a specific blockchain ecosystem. Holders of such tokens receive exclusive benefits such as discounted transaction fees and early access to products and services on the platform.
- → Social tokens: Social tokens are used to monetize engagement on the platform, for example, to reward active supporters of the project for publishing and sharing content. These types of rewards incentivize network participation.
- → Governance tokens: Governance tokens allow the establishment of a blockchain-based voting mechanism by which token-holders can influence the direction of a community. The greater the number of tokens owned, the greater the influence an owner has in the community. It's like democracy but without a government.

> NFTs are part of an evolving ecosystem that's currently being built, and artists have an important role to play in how the technology, systems, and community will ultimately take shape. Get in the habit of showing up for others, making your voice heard, and being generous with your knowledge. LINDSAY HOWARD, FRIENDS WITH BENEFITS

WHAT ARE THESE TOKENS USED FOR?

Social Token — REWARDS USERS OF SOCIAL MEDIA PLATFORMS

Governance Token — PROVIDES TOKEN HOLDERS VOTING RIGHTS

Utility Token — PROVIDES EXCLUSIVE BENEFITS TO HOLDERS

EXAMPLES OF SOCIAL, GOVERNANCE AND UTILITY TOKENS

Cari Social Token — REWARDS CONTENT CREATORS ON THE CHINGARI VIDEO SHARING APP

Maker Governance Token — 1 MAKER TOKEN = 1 VOTE FOR PROPOSALS ON MAKER PLATFORM

Wazirx Utility Token — WAZIRX HOLDERS GET DISCOUNT ON TRADING FEES AND OTHER PERKS

Source: CNBC (2022)

Many people from the non–crypto art world believe that "real art" doesn't need utility, social or governance tokens to keep a community involved and that such art is sufficient in and of itself as a "utility" and to glue a community together. Even the popular project Art Blocks doesn't provide special utility or social tokens to collectors who purchase their art.

But is it really enough to sell just art? Don't forget that artists in the Web3 space are now responsible for marketing their own works, building relationships with collectors and nurturing new ones. Also, it's a key characteristic of the Crypto Art movement to provide "more than just art," as most collectors in the cryptosphere would argue that utility and social recognition matter in the long term. As is the case in the traditional art world, where collectors expect to receive VIP treatment and get invited to exclusive previews,

> **Public auction results have a big signaling power. Use them smartly to establish your brand.** ROMEO BUCHER, ADVISOR, CURATOR

How to build a Web3 Community

NFT collectors have the same expectations.

We believe that finding, onboarding, networking, creating and sustaining a community is critical for NFT success. In order to keep a sense of community alive, NFT projects need to provide constant elements of surprise. It's up to the artist to decide. You can choose to issue NFTs with or without utilities, but we encourage you to be open to enhancing your offer through the use of utility. So let's take a closer look at utility, social and governance tokens.

> Ask yourself, how does this technology serve or amplify the conceptual needs of the work? NANCY BAKER CAHILL, ARTIST

Utility tokens

When we speak of utility tokens, we refer to offerings in addition to the artwork itself. Here are some examples:

→ Airdrops (digital assets distributed directly to community members' wallets free of charge).
→ Early access to new collections.
→ Artist-led studio visits or show openings.
→ Access to exclusive live events.
→ Tickets to virtual meetups.
→ Commercial rights to your NFT, for example, for video games or merchandising.
→ A space to gather in the Metaverse.
→ Physical art.
→ Brand collaborations.
→ Exclusive merchandise.
→ A charity component.
→ An open call for collaborations.
→ A social token launch that includes voting in future projects and partnerships.

Bored Ape Yacht Club (BAYC), a collection to which we have referred frequently, is one of the most successful NFT projects so far. Their NFTs function as membership cards that grant access to members-only benefits—one of which is a private Discord server where you can hang out and chat with other owners. BAYC has started hosting club members at physical events where the celebrity owners will sometimes make appearances. And BAYC NFT holders also own the accompanying commercial use rights. Not only can a BAYC owner resell their NFT for a profit but they can also sell spinoff products based on the art.

Individual artists can offer utility, too. For example, Refik Anadol offers, in addition to the art, physical prints and access to DATALAND, his metaverse project. Artist and curator Kenny Schachter launched his collection of 10,000 CryptoMutts. Buyers get access to Schachter's NFT Arts Club, early access to articles he writes, video lectures and priority minting for future releases of his. Projects such as DAW (Desperate Ape Wives) host collector-only events in different cities, as well as creating partnerships with brands that give collectors first dibs on scooters, coffee or luggage.

> **Identify and engage daily with influential collectors and fellow artists on Twitter and don't hesitate to airdrop your art to them.** DANIEL KROLL, DESPERATE APE WIVES

As you can see, adding value beyond the artwork can contribute to creating a desirable offer. You also don't need to have a large team to manage it. For example, Schachter works mostly on his own. And if you don't want to add events, early access to your next show or studio visits to your NFT, you can always treat the NFT as simply a tool to track your physical or digital artwork to verify exhibition history, loans, movements, international shipping and customs procedures.

Social tokens

Social tokens are the other prominent tokens, although they are not as popular as utility tokens. Social tokens are used to monetize engagement on a platform, for example, to reward active supporters of a project. Each artist, brand, musician, record label, museum or group can launch their own personalized social token that enables them to reward and interact with members of their community. Social tokens provide artists with a means of shaping their own digital economy, enabling them to engage with their fan networks in new and exciting ways. The way a social token can be used will vary from community to community.

Think of social tokens as loyalty programs similar to the ones run by hotels, brands, airlines and coffee chains but, instead of getting useless points, you are rewarded with real money in the form of cryptocurrency. If you go to Starbucks every day and accumulate Starbucks Rewards, you can use them in exchange for menu items. Twenty-five points will get you a free drink; 50 points gets you a free coffee plus a free bakery item; and with 400 points you can start looking at merchandise. However, imagine you decided to stop drinking coffee because of its effect on your digestive system and you wanted to cash out your thousands of points. Cashing out from Starbucks Rewards is not an option, so you would lose those points and your years of loyalty to the company would count for nothing. However, if the loyalty program was in the form of a social token, you could cash out by selling it on the platform.

> It's up to us to create a human experience that makes people happy. JAMES SOMMERVILLE, KNOWN UNKNOWN

Take the example of KnownUnknown, a decentralized creative network created to help creatives connect, collaborate and share with some of the world's most recognizable businesses and projects. Their objective is to revolutionize the typical creative agency using Web3 technology. KnownUnknown invites designers from anywhere in the world to collaborate to pitch campaigns to Fortune 500 companies. Members range from 18 to 87 years old and, regardless of where they come from, they have the same access to opportunities as a 30-year-old living in New York; no one has to get a visa and leave their country to make a living. Everyone is paid using the community's social token, $KUDOS, as a reward for community-building acts such as mentoring and tutoring. This token grants holders benefits such as access to events, one-on-one coaching and other experiences.

> Remember that confidence is like an invisible jacket which is made up from your last experiences. You can put it on to become the artist you are meant to be. EFDOT, ARTIST

Artists can take advantage of social tokens either individually, if they have a strong community, or by uniting with other artists to create collectives. Social tokens can be used in a myriad of ways, including NFT and physical art acquisitions. Artists could host studio visits for token-holders.

Token-holders could be awarded decision-making powers and be invited to contribute to future projects. Artists could pay and reward developers and contributors in tokens, and set up a "token-gated" Discord where token-holders can communicate and where members of the community are authenticated. Other ways of using social tokens include "tokens of appreciation," merch purchases, engage-to-earn, governance, voting, coin-gated exclusive content and access to both physical and digital events. Airdrops are commonly deployed to distribute social tokens to communities and grow the number of token-holders.

Governance tokens (DAO)

Another way of engaging a community is through the use of governance tokens, which give members the right to vote on issues relating to the community. When governance tokens are employed in a community, it is known as a decentralized autonomous organization (DAO). Essentially, DAOs are like decentralized, global companies that are owned by the employees. Unlike traditional companies, DAO are organized not hierarchically but are rather loose and grassroots-driven; decision-making is transparent, and everyone can join globally. As a simple analogy of how they work, imagine you and your friends purchase a barbecue grill together. Each party decides how much money they will contribute to the purchase price. Each party's use of the grill is determined by the amount they put in. Somebody who pays $30 will be able to use the grill three times as much as someone who paid only $10. The same calculation is used in DAOs to determine a member's share of the voting rights. Rules in DAOs are enforced through smart contracts and cannot be changed except through a vote. And governance tokens are the currency that determines the voting rights.

> Find other artists. Many of the greatest artists in the space are approachable through social media, Discord and other real-world events. Artists have supported each other by amplifying others' works or even including their works in their own collection. Creating a creative community around your work is impactful. PRI DESAI, FLAMINGO DAO

How to build a Web3 Community

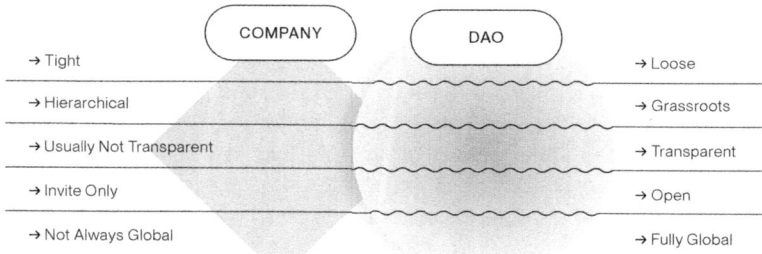

Source: Horowitz (2022)

It's still early days for DAOs, and the ecosystem building the tools for DAOs is just starting to take shape, out of the mainstream. However, the overall philosophy is clear: collective decision-making and less hierarchy; not participants, but owners. DAOs can take on multiple forms and purposes. For example, they can help to fundraise for a project or help make community-led decisions, thereby providing transparent capital flows and allowing everyone to participate in the upside.

> Communicate with your collectors. Give them a place to discuss and mingle with other collectors (or partner with people who can moderate this exchange). DT LUIZ, FINGERPRINTS DAO

DAOs are based solely on communities and their participation. DAOs are structured into the following levels of participants:

- → Level 1: Users – anyone who uses the products or services of the community. There are no gates to enter, and all are encouraged to participate.
- → Level 2: Community members – they influence how the community's products and services are created and disseminated. They are the community's explorers, advocates and evangelists.
- → Level 3: Contributors – these individuals have moved beyond mere membership to become productive assets to the community. Individuals at this level have demonstrated their investment in the community, and their outlook has become more holistic and macro-oriented.
- → Level 4: Teams – this is the level of execution. Teams are the engines of a community, and their ongoing development will define the effectiveness and sustainability of a community's product offering.
- → Team Leads: – These are the champions of a team (e.g., workstream

leaders, project managers, directors). They are not in charge per se, but they are central points of coordination.

Following are some examples of DAOs:

Friends With Benefits FWB is a group of diverse people who advocate for a society in which technology serves as the social connective tissue. They envisage a Web3 future in which data and payments are controlled by the producers. By uniting as a community of creators, rebels, artists, thinkers and doers via a social token—$FWB—members have skin in the game. FWB is creating a membership directory with personalized NFT name badges, preparing a music event, and initiating a fellowship program for minority Web3 artists. In addition, FWB is a platform for music discovery, an online newspaper and a business incubator.

> Ask yourself if what you're creating fundamentally needs to be an NFT. If you can't answer that, it probably shouldn't be one. ALEX ZHANG, FRIENDS WITH BENEFITS

Ukraine DAO Founded by Pussy Riot's political activist Nadezhda Tolokonnikova and digital artists Trippy Labs, Ukraine DAO has raised over $60 million in crypto to fund humanitarian and military initiatives in Ukraine's defense against Russia's invasion. Most of the initiatives are based on the purchase of NFTs of the Ukrainian flag. Support goes to the Ukraine military, displaced families and children caught in the middle of the conflict.

Fingerprints DAO Fingerprints is a DAO that curates and collects artworks and uses smart contracts in exceptionally creative ways. Founded by DT | Luiz in 2019, the main goal of this DAO is to curate, collect and promote on-chain artwork. "On-chain" is the key word, as this means that the NFT is the artwork itself. Most NFTs act as "pointers," where the certificate of provenance is on a public blockchain but the artwork itself is elsewhere. Fully on-chain NFTs are, digitally speaking, the closest you can get to holding a physical artwork.

> The soul of Web3 is about pushing boundaries into new frontiers. Those who take risks, continue to advance the narrative and, above all, remain genuine, are the projects and creators the Web3 industry usually rewards. PLEASR DAO

How to build a Web3 Community

PleasrDAO PleasrDAO is a decentralized community of NFT artists and collectors who have pooled funds to acquire digital art of cultural significance. The DAO was first launched to acquire an NFT created by the artist pplpleasr but swiftly expanded to include more than just pplpleasr's art. The DAO is investigating concepts such as fractionalizing iconic pieces for distribution and community ownership. Their modus operandi is to acquire and support culturally important works, then develop something that fundamentally enhances the essence of the item before returning it to the community.

> How to sell out your art and scale: Start by releasing a small 10 to 20-piece collection, build a Twitter following and community, and recruit collectors and whales to buy your NFT. Then, once you sell out, repeat this model but with a collection size that is 3 to 5 times the size. Then repeat and make sure to do a quarterly valuable gift to all your collectors. REBECCA LAMI, UNICORN DAO

At this point, it might seem too early and complicated for individual artists to create DAOs. We believe, however, that utility, social and governance tokens will shape the future of how artists engage with their communities.

5.5
Communicating With Your Community

Independent of the tokens an artist uses, communication with the community is key. Just as communities of Renaissance artists and collectors would gather at Piazza della Signoria in Florence, crypto communities congregate mainly on Twitter, Discord and Telegram to meet each other, learn and collaborate on projects. Telegram is similar to WhatsApp but is not owned by Meta (Facebook); hence, it is a preferred communication channel. Twitter and Discord, however, are new to many artists (or, at least, they haven't been actively used by them). Let's take a look.

Discord

We have mentioned Discord throughout this book. Discord is the community communication tool most commonly used by the crypto and NFT community. It is an instant messaging and digital distribution platform that allows communities to host phone calls, video calls, text messaging, media and files in private conversations or as part of "server" communities. Think of it as a Slack or Whatsapp but with sub-channels in each group chat to better organize the conversations.

Know that you belong here. You are only claiming your own space as a creative.
MALIHA ABIDI, WOMEN RISE NFT

Your immediate question might be why people are not using WhatsApp or email groups. There are multiple reasons. Discord allows better-organized conversations; it's not owned by Facebook; and the crypto community, which grew out of the gamer culture, brought Discord with it. Discord is what gamers use to livestream their performances and speak to their communities at large.

How to build a Web3 Community

Community managers Most Discord servers employ community managers and moderators ("mods") to build and maintain healthy communities. They also help protect the community from bots and other malicious actors. Many Discord mods started as early token-holders and conversational contributors who demonstrated their passion and interest and are now employed full-time as leaders in the spaces they helped create. This is a great example of how roles are developed within a community.

Token gating Discord Token gating is the process of authenticating community members by limiting server access based on ownership of certain tokens or NFTs. Users can join the Discord channel of any existing NFT project. However, they may not have access to all available channels until they can verify ownership of at least one NFT from the collection. In order to prove that you own the token, you will be prompted to connect your wallet to the channel. If you own the rights, you will then be admitted to the "members-only" chat groups.

> Do extensive research on the most influential projects, artists and platforms in the NFT world. Knowledge is essential. Community is key in supporting each other – it is a completely different crowd to the traditional art world. FEDERICO SOLMI, ARTIST

NFT or social token–holders may have unique benefits that grant access to:

→ NFT holder–only private giveaways.
→ Dedicated and exclusive chat channels for NFT holders.
→ Access to project announcements and previews before the general public is informed.
→ Private live talks or video calls with exclusive content from the artist.

Getting started To get started with Discord, we recommend you first listen in and engage with an existing Discord. The Discord of nft now, for example, is a good starting point as it includes many channels that are open to the public. To enter it, simply visit their website. Clicking on the Discord symbol will open the Discord app (or you will be asked to download it and create a profile). Once you are in their Discord channel, check the vibe and see if it's aligned with your values and if you find the conversations useful. There are millions of Discord channels but only a few are necessary for you. We also recommend you participate—don't just lurk. Introduce yourself and ask questions, give opinions and make statements—obviously according to their code of conduct. Similarly to early Facebook groups, Discord is all about engagement and connecting with each other. So, go ahead and do it.

Twitter

As an artist, you are most likely used to engaging with your community on Instagram, which has emerged over the last five years as the key visual source to find art and connect artists with collectors, other artists and their communities. With NFTs, don't expect to find this community on Instagram. Twitter is where you'll find them, at NFT Twitter. The NFT community initiates talks using a range of hashtags and daily live Twitter Spaces, a rival to (the now almost forgotten) Clubhouse.

> Remind yourself that when you first started making digital art, you did not expect that it would become a hype connected to record sales. Make art again that you think is relevant and contributes to the history of art instead of suddenly worrying about sales. ANIKA MEIER, CURATOR, WRITER

For many, learning about NFTs is as daunting as how to use Twitter, a site that many of us signed up to years ago but then abandoned. Let's review some essential knowledge to help you restart your Twitter journey.

Follow people To get started and fill your Twitter feed, you need to "follow" people. Following will populate your feed with information you will find interesting. Here are 10 accounts you should follow:

- → nft now
- → DeeZe (@Deezefi)
- → RealMissNFT
- → Cozomo de' Medici
- → Andrew Wang (@Andr3w)
- → OhhShiny
- → Anika Meier (@thisaintanika)
- → Jason Bailey (@artnome)
- → Colborn Bell (@colborn)
- → Outland.art

How to build a Web3 Community

Take these as starting points to follow more accounts. The general rule is to follow more people than you feel you need to, as this will enable you to discover more content. And don't worry about getting overloaded. It will happen, but it's normal. The algorithm will make sure you see the most critical tweets.

> Create and lead with your heart and don't be afraid to be your authentic self in this space. Collectors gravitate towards genuine artists and the artist-collector relationships in web3 are very strong and rewarding. DEEZE, COLLECTOR

Hashtags Hashtags facilitate the discovery of Twitter users, discussions and active groups. Experimenting with various hashtags will increase the visibility of your work for those who share your views but are not following you.

Tweet, Engage, Tweak, Repeat In order to connect with people, you need to show that you are active on Twitter. This means you need to reply to a question, tweet, and retweet. I know that many artists prefer to stay in the shadows, but Twitter is all about engagement.

Use DMs to connect You can either see your Twitter direct messages (DMs) as spam or treat them like gold. Think of them as the latter. DMs have become a popular way for followers to ask questions and request whitelists. It's your community's way of engaging with you. Many DMs will be spam, so you will need to filter through those to find valuable contacts.

Social Audio: Twitter Spaces adds depth The audio-based platform Twitter Spaces has developed into an excellent tool to develop your voice and expand your Twitter reach. Think of it as similar to Clubhouse or traditional radio. You may join Twitter Spaces as a speaker, get invited onto a Space as a co-host, or start your own Space as a host. Regardless of your role, you have a unique chance to speak, demonstrate thought leadership and promote your NFT initiative to those who would not have otherwise heard about it. And it's free.

> Don't talk about NFTs. Talk about the value you are offering. ASH POURNOURI, COLLECTOR

The objective of an NFT initiative is to not just reach as many people as possible but also to establish yourself as an expert or leader in your field. Creating and engaging in dialogues in the NFT arena has several advantages, as it provides visibility and credibility to your initiative. Follow Magnus (@magnusresch) and Tam (@TamGZ) on Twitter, as we both host spaces frequently.

Asking your audience questions When working on an NFT project, you must understand what your audience believes. To fulfill the requirements and desires of your community, you must have a thorough understanding of their needs and desires. You must comprehend your audience's likes and dislikes. You must also communicate with them.

> **Your goal should always be to create more value than you extract. Perfect this formula and you've won.** ADAM LEVY, MINT PODCAST

People now want to be able to communicate with the brands, artists and creators they follow. Your NFT pro-ject should give people what they want. Ask them what they want to see from you next, and what they like about your NFTs. The objective is to encourage contact with and participation by the audience. If you do this, you will gather valuable information about your brand's strengths and weaknesses, as well as ideas for future plans for your NFT collections.

●The
Future●●●

The Future

● We are excited about the future of NFTs but we are also realistic, too. Museums of the future won't be crammed with digital screens of punks, apes, and other animals from the zoo.

Picasso's original pieces won't become worthless, selling only if they are turned into NFTs. And not every artist will create a collection of 10,000 utility NFTs. ●●

●6.1●● Structural Changes

We predict that the current convergence of digital art, crypto money and blockchain technology will bring about a profound structural shift in the art ecosystem. We will see changes in traditional purchasing behavior. Collectors won't buy if a work is not registered on the blockchain; creators will exert more control over their work; artists will earn royalties from resales; and the art market will become more regulated, for the better. But, also, new threats and challenges associated with engaging with the NFT market will arise, such as mental health issues.

> Resist the urge to output large quantities of work. In a highly saturated market, strong work stands out. Self-editing can help with this, and being conservative about your output can also help prevent burnout. SINZIANA VELICESCU, VELLUM LA

Below are some thoughts that are merely personal opinions based on experience rather than scientific research. The NFT space might take some turns that lead in a very different direction. So, take these thoughts as inspiration to start thinking about the future of the art market.

Artists Artists' roles have changed throughout the history of the art market. Originally, they were hired as craftsmen to create on-demand works (for churches or wealthy patrons). Eventually, artists organized

The Future

themselves into guilds to promote and protect their work. Galleries then joined the scene to curate and promote selected artists. Looking at the evolution of the role of artists and seeing some of the potential that NFTs bring, we see five major changes:

→ Independence: Today, most artists are introduced to collectors via galleries. We believe that artists will work more independently and not rely on galleries entirely to promote their works.
→ Revenue: As a consequence, artists will earn more on every piece they sell. Traditionally, it's been a 50/50 split with the galleries; in the NFT space, it's a 90/10 split in favor of the artists. So, we will end up somewhere in the middle. Artists will also tap into new revenue streams, for example, converting some of their community into paying members for additional services, unique content or early access. Additionally, they and their heirs will benefit from royalty income.
→ Responsibilities: With increased independence and revenue comes an increase in responsibilities. Whereas artists used to be able to hide behind a gallery, now they are required to deal directly with collectors, the media and incoming requests. For example, they need to respond when collectors have inquiries, are unsatisfied, or want to share their feedback. Art evokes emotion; therefore, artists can expect to be confronted with emotional feedback from their customers. And they will need to reply to requests by the press, curators, museums who want to show their work and more. Some artists today are doing several of these tasks without gallery support. Most artists will, however, hire organizational support to manage their studios, replicating some of the roles you find in traditional galleries today to give them enough space to create art.

> Don't be intimidated by how much there is to learn; we are all learning as much as we can handle, day in and day out. Take time to rest as needed. And, beyond it all, as an artist, learn how to dream in Web3.
> EDWARD ZIPCO, SUPERCHIEF GALLERY

→ Community: Artists will focus more on engaging their communities by allowing them to participate. Rather than just inviting them to shows and engaging in infrequent communication, artists will communicate more openly, frequently and directly with their supporters.
→ Alliances: Without the support of gallerists, artists will rely more than ever on their network to exchange ideas, organize themselves and make use of cross functions. The historic idea of guilds, in which artists were organized according to their craft, might be picked up again and replicated via DAOs – allowing artists to better promote and manage their craft.

Artworks Artworks won't be all digital in the future. Throughout the history of art, paintings have prevailed, and they will continue to do so. Artists won't need a degree in Photoshop or to become AI experts or launch utility collections of 10,000 pieces. However, we believe there will be several changes:

→ Digital twins: Most artists in the physical art space will begin to use NFTs as certificates of authenticity to accompany their work. Whenever a work leaves their studios, artists will upload an NFT of the work to the blockchain. When the work is resold, the NFT will be traded along with it. If an owner does not possess the NFT, they will not be able to resell the art. Artists will also benefit from these "digital twin" NFTs, as they will allow artists to trace the ownership of the work, monitor sales activity, and track royalty earnings.

→ Evolving and interactive artworks: In the digital space, we will see more evolving and adaptable digital artworks, rather than still photographs or short GIFs. An example of this type of art is Daniel Arsham's Eroding and Reforming Bust of Rome (One Year), which decays and disintegrates and then reforms over one year before starting anew at the beginning of the following year. Other digital artworks will interact with the owner, making it a fun hybrid of a game and an artwork. Metaverse Pet Shop, by artist collective Exonemo, is a perfect example. The work shows AI-generated dogs in cages. In remembrance of animals housed in kill shelters, the dogs were offered for sale for $10, disappearing after ten minutes if they were not purchased.

> Your goal should always be to create more value than you extract. Perfect this formula and you've won. ADAM LEVY, MINT PODCAST

→ Prices: We believe that digital art will allow artists to offer works in a new pricing category. Editions have historically been a way for artists to sell lower-priced works; however, the cost of making them has always been high. NFTs allow artists to sell their works at a much lower price point, as almost no production costs are involved. This will expand the price range for artworks in the lower end segment – introducing a new category at around $50, or even free works as special gifts.

Galleries Galleries are the current gatekeepers in the art market. However, the future of their role is in serious doubt. On the one hand, buyers need someone they can trust to recommend pieces—to filter and select the projects to buy from. In this capacity, galleries act more like

The Future

art advisors, working with an extensive roster of artists rather than being bound to a small group of "their own artists." On the other hand, many artists will not want to hire an agent on their own or join artist DAOs, and so will decide to work with a gallery. However, the traditional 50/50 split will not continue. We envisage a more favorable split for artists and also a system that will allow galleries to participate in secondary market royalties (2–10%).

Interesting gallery models with unique approaches to market and sell art have emerged. Quantum Art, Bright Moments, Vellum, Superchief and SuperRare's offline gallery give an idea of where the market might potentially move. These players combine different sales strategies to convert new collectors into buyers of NFTs. Broadly speaking, these sales techniques can be described as:

> Think hard about numerology and a sense of series size / edition numbers. Study the masters of the past like On Kawara and Sol Lewitt. Learn processing to make generative art. Study Herbert Franke and Vera Molnar. Study the history of pixel art. Focus on ongoing levers and triggers to unlock future art drops and other surprises. Create a sense of anticipation and suprise and joy. Create an unique IRL experience for revealing the work with your collector at the same time. SETH GOLDSTEIN, BRIGHTMOMENTS GALLERY

→ Real spaces: All of these platforms have a digital and physical location. They have rented gallery-like spaces to showcase their artists. It's this transition between digital and physical that buyers want to see.
→ Community: In order to get early access to drops, buyers need to become members. These memberships have utilities such as early access to drops, exclusive event invitations, favorable prices and more.
→ Urgency: Most of these galleries create auction-like formats to sell their works. In this way, a format well known from the auction market is retained by the galleries and employed across their digital and physical platforms.
→ Gamification: Buying art can be fun. Bright Moments, for example, experiments with different buying formats. In some of their sales, buyers purchase blindly, not knowing which piece of the collection they will get; in others, they employ a Dutch auction format, creating a fun sense of urgency and competition amongst buyers.

Collectors Collectors will be most impacted by the development of the new art ecosystem. Given that the role of the middleman has shrunk, they will be in closer, more direct contact with artists. There will be more exchanges at the collector level, facilitated by artists. Hence, collectors' networks will expand. It will feel more authentic and, more importantly, we will see more collectors entering the market for the following reasons:

→ Transparency: Collectors will feel more confident buying art because they will know current prices, past prices and comparable prices.
→ Provenance: More collectors will enter the market because information on provenance has become clearer and more accessible. Unclear provenance currently deters many potential buyers from buying art.
→ Liquidity: Selling an artwork in the traditional market is currently very difficult. The NFT sale process is much easier and allows for much faster transactions, demonstrating easier ways to get a return on investments.

Museums Museums will be able to form more lasting relationships with their visitors by engaging with and rewarding them. As a starting point, museum membership programs will be sold as NFTs, thus converting them into smarter versions of loyalty programs. This will lead to the following benefits:

> Know that you belong here. You are only claiming your own space as a creative.
> MALIHA ABIDI, WOMEN RISE NFT

→ Rewards: Museums will be able to reward their most active visitors. The status and relevance of a visitor to a museum will no longer be based solely on the amount they donate but also on how actively they contribute to the institution.
→ New revenue streams: Museums will also be able to tap into new revenue streams. For example, tickets can be sold as special NFT editions for higher prices, artworks from the collection can be converted into NFTs and fractionalized and visitors can buy museum-approved elements for video games or their metaverse rooms.
→ Participation: To retain their members, participation and interaction will be enhanced by giving their community a sense of ownership in the museum. In the long run, museums will play with the idea to allow NFT holders to participate in the curation of selected shows. Rather than only curators deciding what to exhibit, NFT holders will also have a say. Or they might allow their most active members to decide which works

> Better a thousand people who love you than a million people who like you. The latter will chase the next shiny object; the former will know you, defend you, teach you, and give you the patience to shine when the time is right. ANDREW WANG, UNITED TALENT AGENCY

The Future

get purchased and added to the collections. As a benefit of increased participation by their community, a more diverse collection could be established—something museums struggle with.

Naturally, this transition will take time, as museums have historically been slow to adapt to new technologies. We won't see museums flooded with screens, all showing digital artworks. Paintings, sculptures and installations will still be the dominant art form displayed in art museums. Only a few projects out of the current NFT hype are likely to make it into the top museums, thereby guaranteeing their lasting value and also ensuring a record of the early hype around NFT art. Artists, curators and museums will collectively push the limits of how art is displayed.

> **Find ways to make connections with as many of your collectors as possible. Take the time to get to know them and spend time letting them know why you are creating.** GABE WISE, ARTIST

6.2
Regulatory changes

There is no worldwide agreement on NFT legislation at present. Governments and regulatory agencies have been sluggish to classify and control NFTs and other digital assets. This has prevented blockchain technology from expanding more rapidly than it could have. Investors are nervous that governments may arbitrarily outlaw crypto and NFT trading. The central uncertainty is how NFTs might be taxed and controlled in the future. The future of the NFT will be determined primarily by the answer to this question.

> Work work work work work, you big baby. Stay up late every night with your peers. Make an enemy of envy. Otherwise, you die. JERRY SALTZ, ART CRITIC

Taxes

Cryptocurrency and blockchain-based assets are regarded as property by some tax agencies, including the IRS (the U.S. federal tax agency). While the creation of an NFT does not result in a taxable event, its sale would. For example, if an artist sells an NFT for ETH on OpenSea, the revenue would be taxed as regular income. If artists do not convert ETH to USD immediately, a new capital gains holding period begins for the ETH earned from the sale. So, if you sell an NFT, you must report any gain or loss, including if you are compensated in digital currency (which is likely to be the case). This also applies if you sell a gifted NFT, such as an airdrop, for a profit.

> Look for collaborations and don't be afraid to share. Magic will follow! ELENA ZAVELEV, CADAF

Then you will incur capital gains tax and your cost basis will be the original owner's purchase price.

Despite the fact that the crypto tax landscape resembles the Wild West, we expect tax authorities to provide greater guidance eventually.

The Future

Regulations

Experts disagree on whether NFTs can be considered securities, commodities or art. We don't have a definite answer, but here are some thoughts:

Securities are stocks and bonds. People invest in them because they expect their values to rise (or fall, in the case of short selling). In contrast, commodities are physical products such as oil, pigs and corn. In the United States, securities and commodities are governed by distinct government agencies and their regulations. If you want to issue a security, for example, you are subject to these restrictions.

> Read the terms of service of whatever platform you use to know the intellectual property and wallet structures especially. What are you selling—a license or property—and does the platform put your work in a pooled wallet (muddying your digital provenance)? Also, get paid resale royalties and know how your work is being stored—stewarded—long term.
> AMY WHITAKER, PROFESSOR

The question "What can NFTs be used for?" is perhaps the most intriguing component of this categorization debate. NFTs offer a plethora of applications. They are similar to stocks in that they provide investors with the possibility of an appreciating asset. But they also give access to events and other benefits or can serve solely as connections between digital or physical items and their certificates of authenticity. They cannot be consumed, burned, smoked, or handled physically and their potential for extreme price fluctuations adds to the complexity.

Further to the debate, some believe that NFTs should be considered art and, thus, treated similarly to tangible works of art. If treated in this manner, many of the regulatory concerns relating to physical art also apply to NFTs. Three of the most important regulatory concerns in the art industry are as follows:

→ Forgery won't be an issue in the NFT market, as the history of an NFT (its provenance) is tied to the blockchain and cannot be altered.
→ Copyright infringements are a problem in the NFT space, as well as in the traditional market. We have seen an increase in complaints by artists over copyright infringements. NFT platforms will need to develop technologies

to help original creators to protect their copyright.
→ Money laundering is a significant issue in the traditional art market. Therefore, regulators will prioritize tracing the origin of money. Buyers and sellers of NFTs must be prepared to respond to such inquiries.

Recommendations

Given this complex and constantly changing environment of regulations and taxation, what should artists do to stay compliant?

Artists can significantly influence how their NFTs are viewed by considering the language they use when marketing them. For instance, if NFTs are marketed as collectibles, then regulatory authorities may decide that they need not be monitored any more strictly than the sales of traditional collectibles such as baseball cards. In contrast, regulatory authorities would likely have a different view if they saw artists marketing their NFTs as speculative assets that could be traded for a rapid profit.

> Don't listen to Fomo. Pay attention to the people in the space who deliver consistently and have a history of executing projects. KRISTA KIM ARTIST

The degree to which an artist attempts to influence their market is another significant factor in how regulatory authorities will view their work. Is the artist merely selling NFTs to buyers, or are they partnering with a platform or fund to accumulate their own collection of NFTs in addition to the ones they sell? Are they attempting to manipulate the market to increase the value of their own holdings? If artists collecting NFTs and manipulating markets becomes a prevalent practice, authorities may determine that NFT art functions more like a security than a digital figurine or baseball card.

When marketing your NFTs, be wary of celebrity endorsements. The SEC (U.S. Securities and Exchange Commission) has investigated celebrities for promoting securities (such as stocks) on their social media pages without disclosing their links with the companies. According to the rules, if you use celebrities to endorse your products, they must declare their

The Future

affiliation and reveal how much you paid them. If the endorsement is unpaid but the celebrity owns NFTs that you sell, this must also be stated. And be careful about money laundering. It is particularly difficult in the NFT space to know where money is coming from, as many buyers are often unknown or hide behind avatars. When selling on platforms, review their terms and conditions relating to measures against money laundering. This is a rapidly changing area of concern and we expect to see new regulatory developments in the near future.

> **You must be an active promoter as much as a creator. It doesn't matter how innovative and unique your work is if your community does not feel heard.** LEEOR SHIMRON, WRITER

6.3
The Metaverse

"The Metaverse" is one of the most used terms in Web3, yet it's also the least defined. As we have discussed, broadly speaking, it can mean a virtual space where you are able to hang out with friends, work, play, learn, shop, create and more. For artists, the Metaverse can provide unique opportunities as it gives them freedom to create in an environment where there are no boundaries. Here are some ideas to get you dreaming:

> NFTs expose the art market's insularity, elitism, opacity and relative lack of regulation. Don't be scared. Embrace it.
> TOM FLYNN, ART PROVENANCE RESEARCH AGENCY

NFTs are everywhere NFTs will potentially become the keys to the Metaverse. Everything will be an NFT: your ID, property, houses, clothes, avatars, the environment and, of course, your art. NFTs are how we protect our IP in the Metaverse. You will be able to enter different rooms, events and places in the Metaverse using NFTs and social tokens which will serve as the gating and authentication mechanisms. Your art will only participate in the Metaverse if it's an NFT.

Art for everyone Concerts and events will take place in the Metaverse, making use of its unlimited space. Galleries, museums and art fairs will have their own spaces, host events, invite people and organize talks. The concept is similar to online viewing rooms (OVR), but the environment will be more entertaining and inviting. And it will bring artists into contact with new buyers. It is possible that the physical-world experience will become more niche and luxurious while the Metaverse becomes more democratic and accessible for all.

> Investors and collectors alike are looking for a unique value proposition: some combination of innovation (pushing NFT use-cases forward) and upside potential from capital appreciation. Authenticity and execution are, therefore, of the utmost importance. BRANDON BUCHANAN, META 4

Infinite creative possibilities There are no constraints when it comes

The Future

to building in the Metaverse. There is no gravity, no wall that is too big (or small), no material that needs taming, no manufacturing constraints. Artists can create their wildest dreams—flying shoes, clothes on fire, liquid bodies, shirts with holograms and songs—anything is possible in the Metaverse.

> I see little difference between a successful NFT project and a valuable traditional art object or exhibition. What is the worthy intention and utility? What is the message? Where is the passion? What makes it relevant and unique? Does it push both the medium, conversation, technology and human species forward in a positive manner? If so, you're poised for success. KURT MCVEY, WRITER

Bionic hardware Hardware will develop in such a way that it becomes easier to have a physical experience using the Metaverse. We will be able to use it to touch, smell and taste things. For example, we will be able to visit an artist's studio and smell the colors and the sense of freshly painted works when the canvas is still wet. And we will be able to touch a work (yes, no security guards in sight). Obviously, this sounds futuristic, but as we said, we wanted to get you dreaming.

Community building A little less dreamy are our views on community building in the Metaverse. Your collectors will engage with you and your metaverse and earn points for their interaction. They will come to participate in votes and influence decisions. Most metaverses have their own social tokens used for governance, to reward their communities for contributions, world-building and trading of digital assets.

Self-expression Communities will thrive on a completely expansive idea of self-expression and will actively build alternate versions of reality. We all create our own avatars and characters based on our alter egos and fantasies. Those avatar NFTs will become our digital identities. Aesthetics, personality, expression and ownership will be reinvented.

> Always think of how you can leave this space better than you found it. Be part of the revolution as well as the evolution. EMILY LAZAR, ARTIST

6.4 Risk

Naturally, with immense opportunities come risks. We have already talked extensively about the risk of fraud, copyright infringements, speculations, volatility, price inflation and storage issues with IPFS. The following sections highlight some scenarios that may become more relevant.

Centralization

As is the case with any new technology, there is always the risk that opportunists will take the crypto ethos—which is based on decentralization, permissionlessness and global technology—in an unhealthy direction that will harm the participants.

The potential of the Metaverse is that all of our digital lives may eventually take place inside it. Think of a future in which we do everything digitally in the Metaverse, including using it as a place to work, exercise, learn and shop. This scenario brings with it a tremendous risk of centralization. Imagine if Meta (which already owns your IP and uses it as revenue for advertising) acquired even more data related to your entire life, including your work, workout routines and shopping patterns. They would make it easy for their users to mint NFTs and transition into the Metaverse, using all the content that their users have already created on Instagram, WhatsApp and Facebook. While this won't have an immediate impact on artists, such a scenario would be a dystopia from a crypto native's perspective.

> Do thorough research of the NFT landscape and its mechanisms (from smart contracts and platforms to environmental impact) before you get involved, and don't hang JPEGs on the blockchain, but use it as a medium. CHRISTINE PAUL, PROFESSOR, CURATOR

The Future

Market downturns

The markets are seasonal, and Web3 is no exception. It's inherently volatile, as we have seen in the May/June 2022 downturns. Spectacular increases in 2021 have drawn throngs of amateur and professional investors, all seeking a fast return. Many of them ride an upswing and then exit to take a profit, or they sell in a hurry when conditions deteriorate, thus realizing their loss. You often then hear the term "Crypto Winter", meaning a prolonged period characterized by a sustained general drop in the prices of digital assets which, in turn, hinders enthusiasm for the entire industry.

> **Web3 is all about creativity, community and utility—each component is equally important for any successful NFT project to stand the test of time.** SHANYAN KODER, COLLECTOR

Summer gives way to winter's frost, and winter thaws in summer's heat. When the dust settles, the advancements achieved by builders during difficult times rekindle hope. Some blockchain companies, cryptocurrencies, creators and NFT projects can survive a bearish winter, while others will not have the confidence, resources or strength to do so. Downturns are useful events, in that they serve to flush opportunists and unsustainable projects from a market. Unfortunately, however, many innocent investors, builders, employees and supporters are also hurt by downturns.

Marketing and investment in the Web3 space moves much faster than the development of the engineering and infrastructure needed to sustain Web3's long-term vision. Artists should keep this in mind and do their due diligence instead of falling blindly in love with any given creative technology at the edge of innovation. But, also, don't turn away too early. Consider that potential entrepreneurs who swore off the internet in the wake of the dotcom disaster of the early 2000s missed the decade's biggest opportunities: cloud computing, social networks, online video streaming, cellphones. The next big projects are often built during a downturn.

> **Focus on building a solid community first. NFTs can be a way to energize that community, but won't necessarily be enough to create that community on their own.** EMILY PARKER, COINDESK

Mental health

As the Metaverse emerges, we will spend even more time in front of a screen. As digital tools become more prevalent, we must learn to be more disciplined about limiting our exposure to technology. So much of the feedback we receive from artists is about the risks and fears related to technology consuming our lives. Are humans rapidly becoming cyborgs and avatars? Where is the place for creativity and art, then? Where do we get our inspiration from? It is up to us to be disciplined about mental health. The following advice is given based on what has worked for us.

> You slowly accrue recognition by repeating your message over and over and over; so make sure that message is something you'll believe in for a long time — not just a passing trend. MITCHELL F. CHAN, ARTIST

Sleep in a different room from your electronics When you first wake up in the morning, your brain shifts from delta waves, which are associated with a profound sleep, to theta waves, which are associated with a type of daydreaming state. Your brain produces alpha waves when you are awake, calm, and not processing a great deal of information. Avoid looking at your phone! If you jump straight into using a device, you will push your brain to bypass the crucial theta and alpha phases and proceed directly from the delta stage to a state of heightened alertness.

Wellness If you have never done any wellness practices before, right now is the time to explore breathwork, meditation, yoga, ecstatic dance, reiki, Pilates, sound baths or any cathartic calming practice.

> I would share the Brechtian maxim, addressed to his friend Walter Benjamin: "Don't start with the good old stuff but with the bad news." That is the best advice I can give. PROFESSOR YUN, ART CRITIC

Meeting choices Anytime you can meet someone face-to-face rather than on Zoom or in the Metaverse, choose to meet them in person. Anytime you can hold a meeting while walking outdoors, choose that option. Appreciate the real world around you. Listen to music. Experience physical art. Spend time outdoors every day.

The Future

Spend time with loved ones Spend time daily with your friends and family, in person. Schedule time into your routine for contact with your favorite humans, plants and animals. The Metaverse will challenge us to spend more and more time in the digital world. We will need to break this pattern. Be mindful about every task. Shower, eat and dress slowly. Don't try to multitask while using tech.

> New technologies can help reduce the inequities in the art world. Web3 has the potential to open new channels for sales and community-building but it will be up to artists to get educated and to protect themselves, especially their intellectual property rights in this new frontier.
> DEXTER WIMBERLY, CURATOR

Create no-tech zones Keep areas of your home free from technology. No-tech zones can include the dinner table and the bedroom. Keep areas of your schedule blocked off as no-tech times. These can include focus time, writing time, studio time, brainstorm time, mornings, workout time, wellness time, family and friends time and sleep time. Use airplane mode often, and create clear boundaries.

Privacy You have the right and responsibility to create, maintain and protect a balance between online presence and what you decide to share with others. You can check out from your online identity anytime and at any point. You do not owe anyone any explanations. There will always be messages and notifications waiting, so don't wait for them to be dealt with before taking a break. You don't need to earn a break from technology in order to take it.

> Prioritize your mental health and well-being. It's a marathon, not a race. Say no to projects that do not align with your values and your purpose. Trust yourself and never lower your standards.
> OLIVE ALLEN, ARTIST

To sum it all up, the most effective way to safeguard our mental health is to constantly prioritize doing something good for other people. That was one of the key reasons we decided to write this book. It has been a rewarding exercise for us.

●Conclusion●●●

Conclusion

● "Is it art?" asked one critic. "All of these people really amuse us, but the annoying thing is that none of them are worthy of the title 'artist.' It's a con, a hoax, and endangering art history and the whole aesthetic tradition." ●●

What sounds like something that might have been said during a debate in 2022 about NFTs was actually said in 1940 when art reviewers were discussing an Art Brut display. However, the critics of today sound identical in their condemnation of NFTs and their characterization of Crypto Art as a fad—a bubble, a modern version of tulip mania. Obviously, not everyone is excited about the prospect of change in the art industry. But, don't forget, digital art encompasses a wide variety of techniques that stretch back at least to the 1960s.

> Community and utility are the cornerstones of a good project. If you focus on these aspects, the financial component will follow. The power of Web3 lies in putting the power back in the artist's hands and the connection he can have with those who support him. Create an ecosystem that goes beyond the art itself.
> ALEX HALL, THE CHAINSMOKERS

We think that the introduction of NFTs and the various ways of using them has the potential to change the market in a way that could not have been accomplished otherwise. It is the collaboration, co-creation, and dialogue between artists, engineers, and the audience that makes this transitional phase between institutionalized "painting and sculpture" tradition and digital art so dominant.

Conclusion

The new way of working is laying bare the insularity, elitism and opaqueness of the traditional art market.

Does this mean the art market will change entirely tomorrow and all its players will vanish? Definitely not, because changes in the art world take time. And because the inner sanctum of the art market will surely endure, relying as it does on established relationships. Does that, then, mean that Picassos will be replaced by digital art and MFA programs will mostly graduate digital artists? Also, no. Painting is not dead, and digital art as a medium will continue to constitute a small share of the market. And does that mean that gallerists and curators will become entirely obsolete? Certainly not.

> Less looking out and more looking in, all the answers you need as an artist are inside you. The artist lives for their vision and their vision alone; the world doesn't know what they need until you give it to them, so it's imperative to know yourself and to continue diving deeper within and expressing outward. The world so desperately needs a mirror, and only the artists who have truly searched themselves can provide that. DRIFT, ARTIST

We believe that the advantages of NFTs and blockchain technology will contribute to a better art market, one that is fairer and more equal and democratic. A market that is more inviting, less exclusive and more transparent—converting a large number of new visitors into buyers who purchase art. Art institutions can benefit tremendously from the new capabilities that NFTs and their underlying technologies give us by better engaging their communities and giving them ownership through participation and involvement in governance.

This shift toward more independence for artists also means more responsibilities. In a world where collectors communicate directly with the artists, who is selling the works, then, when the artist is busy creating? In order to sustain this shift, artists will need to become more entrepreneurial and learn to manage new tasks. Some will hire more staff, others will gladly work with galleries that take on the jobs of selling, promoting, placing and supporting—the roles that galleries today are already

> Find creative ways to engage your new NFT-collecting patrons. Keep them happy and you'll create an independent source of funding with which to escape dependence on the old gatekeepers of culture. MICHAEL CASEY, COINDESK

performing. But the power dynamics will have switched.

The writing is on the wall. You are early, and we congratulate you on reading this book. So, don't worry: Nostradamus-like predictions of the gradual decline of the traditional art world into antiquity may be slightly premature. We're simply entering a new era. By reading this book, you are taking the steps to embrace change. The future is what you choose to make of it.

> Artists have a beautiful way of seeing the world on their own terms and sharing that vision with an audience. This is a special time for artists to bring their unique perspective and leverage blockchain technology for their art, as their art, and as the medium for social commentary.
> MICHELLE ABBS, WEB3 EQUITY

Further Reading & References

Further reading & references

● There is so much to read and learn in the crypto space that it can be overwhelming. Below are a few resources we recommend to listen, read and watch. Take these as a starting point in your journey to enhance the learning about the NFT space.

We have also added a few key terms that are frequently used, so you can feel confident when speaking to others. ●●

● 8.1 ● ●
Top Resources

Podcasts:

→ nft now by Matt Medved, Alejandro Navia, Sam Hysell
→ Proof by Kevin Rose
→ Mint by Adam Levy
→ Overpriced JPGs by Carly Reilly

Newsletters to subscribe to:

→ Bankless
→ nft now
→ Metanews by Metaversal
→ Real Vision
→ Greg Insenberg
→ NFT Lately
→ NFT Culture
→ Building the Metaverse
→ Ryan Schultz
→ Nonfungible.com
→ NFT + Coffee

Further reading & references

Videos to watch:

→ a16z Crypto Startup School

More Twitter accounts to follow:

→ @TinaRiversRyan
→ @0xdesigner
→ @farokh
→ @ph0enixwilder
→ @decenarts
→ @cdixon
→ @cosomomedici
→ @museumofcrypto
→ @aoristart
→ @_____jpg_____

8.2
Top Crypto Terms

Ape / Aping Aping is the act of purchasing a crypto asset without much investigation or consideration. You just go with the flow. You click the "buy" button because the purchase seems right.

Airdrop NFTs may be "airdropped" between crypto wallets in the same manner that files can be "airdropped" between iPhones. Typically, this occurs within the framework of an NFT project that is sending extra NFTs or tokens to current holders as a reward for their loyalty or an encouragement to participate further.

Allowlist Due to the competitive nature of NFT drops, some projects may form a "allowlist" (also known as a "whitelist"). This allows you to mint before the general public.

Bots Programs that conduct particular activities automatically are known as "bots." Frequently, bots are used improperly to spam accounts with ads for new projects. Another kind of bot might provide a variety of modifications for Discord servers, such as answering frequently asked questions, providing mini-games to their community or generating memes every day.

Floor Price Similar to a low estimate at an auction, the floor price is the cheapest price for which a certain NFT may be purchased. A floor price that is higher than the mint price shows that a project is in demand; conversely, a floor price that is lower than the mint price is often a negative investment signal.

GM Good morning. Constantly used by Twitter users when greeting each other.

HODL "Hold on for dear life." (Pronounced "hod-el.") Often used as a rallying cry on Twitter when the floor price of a project increases or decreases. The expression essentially means "Maintain your composure; don't panic."

Further reading & references

PFP Used as an acronym for "profile pictures". "PFP" often refers to a project that has little utility beyond its function as a social media avatar. The most prominent ones are CryptoPunks and Bored Apes. PFP projects are often issued in editions of 10,000, with each NFT possessing unique properties.

Mods Twitter or Discord channel moderators are referred to as "mods." Moderators are responsible for ensuring healthy, engaging, and instructive community experiences in these spaces.

WAGMI "We're all gonna make it." Typically used in an exclamatory style on Twitter to emphasize that a project "will be successful." Can also be used to encourage doubters to maintain optimism in a failing project. The opposite expression is "NGMI" ("not going to make it").

On-chain On-chain transactions are blockchain-based transactions that are recorded on a public, decentralized ledger.

8.3
References in this book

Anvesh.eth [@anveshreddy]. (2021, October 12). *Starting a thread with all beginner guides, 101 type of content for web3, nfts, crypto...* [Tweet]. Twitter. https://twitter.com/anveshreddyj/status/1447613017038868482?s=24

Artsy. (2022). Artsy Gallery Insights: 2022 Report. Artsy. https://partners.artsy.net/resource/2022-gallery-insights-report/

ArtTactic/Hiscox. Hiscox online art trade report 2021 (Part 1). Hiscox & ArtTactic. https://www.hiscox.co.uk/sites/default/files/documents/2021-10/21674a-Hiscox_online_art_trade_report2021-part_one_1.pdf

Beckman, M. (2021). The Comprehensive Guide to NFTs, Digital Artwork, and Blockchain Technology. Simon and Schuster.

Chainalysis. (2022). The Chainalysis 2021 NFT Market Report. Chainalysis. https://go.chainalysis.com/nft-market-report.htm

Chow, A. R. (2021, March 22). NFTs are shaking up the art world—but they could change so much more. Time. https://time.com/5947720/nft-art/

CNBC-TV18. Social Tokens Vs. Governance Tokens Vs. Utility Tokens. CNBC-TV18. https://www.cnbctv18.com/cryptocurrency/social-tokens-vs-governance-tokens-vs-payment-tokens-13396692.htm

Conti, R., & Schmidt, J. (2022, April 8). What is an NFT? Non-fungible tokens explained. Forbes Advisor. https://www.forbes.com/advisor/investing/cryptocurrency/nft-non-fungible-token/

Dixon, C. (2018, February 18). Why decentralization matters. cdixon.org. https://cdixon.org/2018/02/18/why-decentralization-matters

Further reading & references

Fraiberger, S. P., Sinatra, R., Resch, M., Riedl, C., & Barabási, A. L. (2018). Quantifying reputation and success in art. Science, 362(6416), 825–829.

Galloway, S. (2022, March 29). The Real Potential of NFTs. Medium.com. https://marker.medium.com/the-real-potential-of-nfts-b1bf88b24a1c

Geroni, D. (2021, September 1). Understanding the attributes of non-fungible tokens (NFTs). 101blockchains.com. https://101blockchains.com/nft-attributes

Graves, F. (2022, February 20). Sorry, Your NFT Is Worthless: The Copyright and Generative Art Problem for NFT Collections. IPWatchdog. https://www.ipwatchdog.com/2022/02/20/sorry-nft-worthless-copyright-generative-art-problem-nft-collections/id=146163/

Gryn, T. (2021, October 12). Digital Art and Duchamp's Fountain: How Reflections of Society Spur the Biggest Controversies. Decentralized Arts #8 October 11. https://banklessdao.substack.com/p decentralized-arts-8-october-11?r=elwu6&s=r

Hoffman, D. (2021, September 2). The Metaverse Emerges. Bankless [newsletter]. https://newsletter.banklesshq.com/p/the-metaverse-emerges?utm_source=url&s=r

Horowitz, A. (2022). The State of Crypto: an overview report. a16z crypto. https://a16zcrypto.com/state-of-crypto-report-a16z-2022/
Infinite Objects (n.d). What does it mean to "print" an NFT? https://support.infiniteobjects.com/hc/en-us/articles/4405775599252-What-does-it-mean-to-print-an-NFT-

Little, K. (2022, April 18). What is blockchain and how does it work? NextAdvisor/Time. https://time.com/nextadvisor/investing/cryptocurrency/what-is-blockchain/

McAndrew, C. (2022). The Art Market 2022: An Art Basel & UBS Report [Art Market Report]. Art Basel & UBS. https://artbasel.com/about/initiatives/the-art-market

Nakamoto, S. (2008). Bitcoin: A peer-to-peer electronic cash system. Decentralized Business Review, 21260.
https://bitcoin.org/bitcoin.pdf

NonFungible.com. (2022). NFT Market Quarterly Report: Q1 2022. NonFungible.com.
https://nonfungible.com/reports/2022/en/q1-quarterly-nft-market-report

Raustiala, K., & Sprigman, C. (2021, November 24). Tarantino vs. Miramax — Behind the NFT 'Pulp Fiction' Case, and Who Holds the Advantage. The Hollywood Reporter.
https://www.hollywoodreporter.com/business/digital/tarantino-miramax-pulp-fiction-nft-1235052378/

Resch, M. (2018). Management of Art Galleries. Phaidon.
https://www.magnusresch.com/books/

Resch, M. (2021). How To Become A Successful Artist. Phaidon.
https://www.magnusresch.com/books/

Rodeck, D., & Curry, B. (2022, April 28). What is blockchain? Forbes Advisor.
https://www.forbes.com/advisor/investing/cryptocurrency/what-is-blockchain/

Roy, A. (2022, April 4). Former Head Of Design At Coca-Cola Aims To Reinvent the Creative Agency. Entrepreneur India.
https://www.entrepreneur.com/article/423792

Taggart, E. (2018, January 18). How the pioneers of pointillism continue to influence artists today. My Modern Met.
https://mymodernmet.com/pointillism-art-georges-seurat/

Vasan, K., Janosov, M., & Barabási, A. L. (2022). Quantifying NFT-driven networks in crypto art. Scientific reports, 12(1), 1-11.
https://www.nature.com/articles/s41598-022-05146-6Beckman, M. (2021).

Experts

Here is a list of experts who contributed to this book. We are grateful for every expert and their advice.

Interviews
Some interviews can be watched on magnusclass.com (for a fee)

Aaron Huey
Adam Levy
Adam Lindemann
Alejandro Navia
Alex Hall
Alex Zhang
Ali Spagnola
Amanda Cassatt
Amanda Fairey
Amber Vittoria
Amy Whitaker
An Rong
Andrew Wang
Anika Meier
Aniko Berman
Anne Morgan Spalter
Ash Pournouri
Ashley Ramos
Audrey Ou
Ben Gentilli
Brandon Buchanan
Brian Chambers
Brian Mark
Caroline Taylor
Chris Adamo
Christine Paul
Ciphrd

Claire Silver
Colborn Bell
Cory Van Lew
Damjanski
Dan Mikesell
Daniel Kroll
Daniel Rosenberg
Dave Krugman
Deeze
Derek Anderson
Dexter Wimberly
Dmitri Cherniak
Dot Pigeon
Drift
DT Luiz
Duncan Cock Foster
Edward Zipco
Efdot
Elav Horwitz
Elena Zavelev
Emily Lazar
Emily Parker
Eric Young
Federico Solmi
FEWOCiOUS
Feyyaz Alingan
Gabe Wise

Experts

Gianni Lee
Gizem Saka
Gmoney
Hackatao
Holly Wood
Ix shells
J.N Silva
Jaclyn Lavy
James Sommerville
Jasmine Maietta
Jen Stark
Jenkins the Valet
Jenni Thompson
Jerry Saltz
Jesse Lee
Joe Kennedy
Johann Koenig
John Cain
Josh Rosenthal
Justin Aversano
Justin Melillo
Karen Levy
Kasey
Kat Cohen
Kayvon Tehranian
Keith Grossman
Kennedy Yanko

Kenny Schachter
Krista Kim
Kurt McVey
Leeor Shimron
Lesley Silverman
Lindsay Howard
Luisa Ausenda
Maliha Abidi
Marisa Sechrest
Martin Lukas Ostachowski
Matthew Liu
Mauricio Figueroa
Megan Kaspar
Meltem Demirors
Micah Johnson
Michael Bouhanna
Michael Casey
Michelle Abbs
Micol Apruzzese
Mike Darlington
Mike Dudas
Mitchell F. Chan
Nancy Baker Cahill
Nanne Dekking
Nato Thompson
Noah Davis

Olive Allen
Oxb1
Pablo Rodriguez-Fraile
Paul Cossu
Pauline Foessel
Peter Wu
Pleasr DAO
Pri Desai
Professor Yun
QuHarrison Terry
Rachel Rossin
Rahilla Zafar
Raj Gokal
Rebecca Lamis
Richerd Chan
Romeo Bucher
Roxy Fata
Sam Schoonover
Samantha James
Sarah Meyohas
Sarah Odenkirk
Sarah Zucker
Sasha Stiles
Seneca
Seth Goldstein
Shantell Martin
Shanyan Koder

Sian Morson
Sinziana Velicescu
Skot Leach
Snowfro
Sofia Garcia
Sparky
Steven Sacks
Studio Drift
Swan Sit
ThankYouX
The Haas Brothers
Tom Flynn
Trevor Jones
Wolf Lieser
Yoram Roth
Zelika Garcia

About the authors

Magnus Resch, PhD, is an art market economist, serial entrepreneur, and bestselling book author. He teaches art management at Yale, and has previously taught at Columbia. In 2016, he launched the Magnus app, which works like Shazam for art. Leonardo DiCaprio is an investor and adviser to the company. Magnus holds a PhD in economics, and studied at Harvard, the London School of Economics, and the University of St. Gallen. He has written seven books on the art market and his career has been portrayed in a Harvard Business School case study and in various articles, including in the *New York Times, Wall Street Journal, Vanity Fair,* and *Financial Times.* Magnus can be reached at magnus@magnusresch.com or via Instagram and Twitter (@magnusresch).

Tam Gryn is the former director of fine arts at Rally.io, where she helped artists create their own autonomous crypto economies, as well as head curator at SHOWFIELDS, where she is bridging art with retail. Tam has lectured at Harvard Business School and the New York Academy of the Arts. She currently contributes to Decentralized Arts by BanklessDAO and Women in Web3 Equity Miami. She was formerly the head of the curatorial department of the Artist Pension Trust as well as head curator for RAW POP UP, and was the founder of Culturadora. Tam sits on the board of the Kulturespace Foundation in Berlin. Originally from Venezuela, she studied Art History at Sorbonne University. She then specialized in Politics and Diplomacy at the Reichman University in Israel and received her M.A. in Negotiation and Conflict Resolution from Tel Aviv University. Tam can be reached via Twitter and Instagram.

Imprint

Magnus Books
174 West 4th Street
NY 10014 New York
United States
magnusresch.com

Authors
Magnus Resch & Tam Gryn

Copy Editor
Rollin Kennedy

Design
Karolina Rosina-Meisen
www.thegentletemper.com

ISBN 979-8-218-01153-6
First edition published in June, 2022 ©

American Library of Congress Control N
2022910820

All rights reserved. No part of this public
may be reproduced, stored, in a retrieval
or transmitted, in any form or by any mea
electronic, mechanical, photocopying, re
or otherwise, without written permission.

Printed in Great Britain
by Amazon